INSTEAD
OF
DEATH

books by WILLIAM STRINGFELLOW

An Ethic for Christians and Other
Aliens in a Strange Land

A Second Birthday

Dissenter in a Great Society

Free in Obedience

My People is the Enemy

A Private and Public Faith

Count it all Joy

with ANTHONY TOWNE

The Death and Life of Bishop Pike

Suspect Tenderness

The Bishop Pike Affair

NEW AND EXPANDED EDITION

INSTEAD OF DEATH

William Stringfellow

Wipf & Stock
PUBLISHERS
Eugene, Oregon

Wipf and Stock Publishers
199 W 8th Ave, Suite 3
Eugene, OR 97401

Instead of Death
New and Expanded Edition
By Stringfellow, William
Copyright©1963 by Stringfellow, Wiliam
ISBN: 1-59244-873-9
Publication date 9/24/2004
Previously published by The Seabury Press, 1963

for POLLY

Foreword to the 2004 Edition

The publication of these volumes, first in a reviving series of William Stringfellow's remarkable corpus, couldn't come at a more welcome moment. This, not only because the appearance roughly marks the twenty year anniversary of his death, March 2, 1985, but because their clear-eyed prescience will serve Christians and others in the current historical moment. These were important books when they were written, and may actually prove even more so now. As Karl Barth, the great German theologian, once quipped to an audience regarding Stringfellow, "You should listen to this man!" It is not too late to heed him.

Of his sixteen books, these three—*An Ethic for Christians and Other Aliens in a Strange Land, Conscience and Obedience,* and *Instead of Death*—comprise something of an ethics trilogy. Stringfellow himself regarded the first two in such a relationship (anticipating another unfinished at his death) and the latter serves well to suggest a sequence. In their present form these books were published within a term of four years (1973–1977), a tumultuous period in U.S. politics covering the end of the war in Southeast Asia, the collapse of the Nixon presidency under the weight of Watergate, the elaborate mythic ritualization of the Bicentennial celebration, and the emergence of what Stringfellow termed "technocratic totalitarianism."

Because his ethics are sacramental and

incarnational, advocating discernment of the Word within the contestations of history, mentioning those events is not incidental. What remains so striking is that his uttered vision in that moment and from that vantage should peer so deeply and precisely into our own. These books fall open as to the present, unsealing the signs of our own times. Technocratic totalitarianism indeed.

Because he urges a biblical ethic which is rooted in vocation—thus implicating our lives, our biographies, and our identities in the Word of God—it is equally apropos to mention his own involvements in this period. Stringfellow was then living with his partner, Anthony Towne, on Block Island off the Atlantic coast where he kept something of a monastic regimen, and was active in town politics. Having recently survived life-threatening illness, he remained a permanent, if vigorous, invalid—managing throughout to travel, speak, and write with great authority. He was certainly the subject of government surveillance in these years, having recently been indicted for "harboring a fugitive," namely his friend, the anti-war priest and poet Daniel Berrigan. In this same period, moreover, he himself had called for the impeachment of President Nixon, prior to Watergate and on the basis of war crimes. Meanwhile on the churchly front, he served as canonical counselor and defender of the first Episcopal women priests irregularly ordained.

Years prior he had been an international leader in the postwar ecumenical student movement, and in that connection first heard tell of the "principalities and powers" in the sober witness of those emerging from the confessional resistance movements of Europe. That theological insight was verified by his own experience in

New York's East Harlem ghetto where, after graduation from Harvard Law School in 1956, he took up residence to practice and improvise street law. His neighbors spoke openly of the police, the mafia, the welfare bureaucracy, even the utility companies as though they represented the power of death—predatory creatures arrayed against the community. Stringfellow took the clue biblically. He ran with the book.

No theologian in the United States did more, though generally uncredited, to bring the biblical view of the "powers" back onto the map of hermeneutics and theological ethics. Each of these volumes, in different ways, reflects that effort. This includes naming the power of death as a living moral reality and recognizing it, in the era of the fall, as the very power behind the powers.

Each of them also variously bespeaks Stringfellow's concern for the Constantinian captivity of the church—and with it, side by side, the moral justification of the nation as divinely sanctioned. He beheld the theological elaborations of "America" as the justified, elected, and righteous empire to be a form of blasphemy. Yet if anything, in our own moment, empire has been more openly embraced than ever as a divinely authorized vocation, a presumption of historical sovereignty, a manichean mission in the world of both global terror and corporate globalization. If for none but that reason alone, these pages light up our own moral landscape.

Instead of Death was the only book of Stringfellow's republished in his lifetime. Since, as in the present edition, it was expanded to include additional material, it is something of a remarkable hybrid, being written in two distinctive moments of his life and, in a certain sense, with two different audiences in mind. I read the original 1962 edition as an adolescent in the mid sixties, part of the audience for which the high school study pamphlet version was first intended. That material deals with issues like loneliness, sexuality, identity, and work—all concerns of adolescents—but written without condescension, without masking the work of the powers hid therein, and without sacrificing the rigors of his radically paradoxical theological method. In consequence, that reading marked for me the first time I "thought theologically." His treatment may be so straightforward, in part, because these were also issues of immediate concern in his own biography. In 1961, for example, he was in fact deeply lonely. So he knows the grace and freedom to which he testifies.

The expanded material includes a remarkable preface, an essay worth the price of the book, in which he reflects on the earlier edition from a standpoint twenty-five years subsequent. This calls up, among other things, thoughts on what it means to live biblically, on the idolatry of ethical consistency, and the false distinction between the personal and the political. It is here that he credits the East Harlem residents of putting him onto the principalities and so enabling him in the freedom of the resurrection to transcend prolonged and debilitating illness in his own life. The additional chapters move seamlessly from the original meditation on work, to a critique of the commercial principalities in consumer culture, and finally into his most concise and devastating analysis of our totalitarian technocracy, regnant today. The resistance ethic commended is that implicit in the original title: an ethic of resurrection.

It is to be expected that some will find these volumes somber, dark, and theologically gloomy. So be it. Such times are our own. They remain, nevertheless, the most hopeful books I have ever read. They name the militant activity of the Word of God, present and efficacious, in the darkest of historical circumstance. Stringfellow had the gift to look the beast in the eye and, in faith, neither flinch nor fail. The realism of his gaze is inseparable from true Christian hope. So much else is denial, wishdream, and hope gone cheap. May the reappearance of these volumes summon us simultaneously to the truth of our times and living of that hope.

Feast of All Saints 2004
Bill Wylie-Kellermann

Contents

Otherwise, what do people mean by being baptized on behalf of the dead? If the dead are not raised at all, why are people baptized on their behalf?

I Corinthians 15:29

INSTEAD
OF
DEATH

Preface

In 1962 the Christian Education Department of the Executive Council of the Episcopal Church asked me to write a book for adolescents to be included in its curriculum for high school youth. My compliance with that invitation was a short studybook entitled *Instead of Death*.

The manuscript evoked controversy before it was ever published. To start with, the title I had decided upon was considered a deterrent to the book's reader appeal. I was told that no one would look at a book with "death" in the title. However, I was stubborn and the book was published without compromising my title. The fear that the use of the word "death" would hamper the sales of *Instead of Death* proved to be unwarranted. The book has sustained a very wide circulation, and since its publication, death has become a topical issue in America. It is the subject of innumerable courses in schools and colleges, a central theme in political discourse, a stock issue for television panels, and a matter of sudden interest in the fields of medicine and psychology.

I claim neither originality nor foresight in attempting to deal, at the time I wrote *Instead of Death,* with some of the meanings of the presence of death. Biblical people have always had such a concern and, indeed, have characteristically claimed a peculiar comprehension of death as a moral power affecting every aspect of human existence in this world. At the same time, death is not a morbid preoccupation in biblical faith, such as it may have now become in American society. The focus of the biblical witness is not upon death as such, but upon the historic transcendence of death—upon the resurrection from death. It was this relation of the power of death to the word of God, this saga of death *and* resurrection, this simultaneous attention to the awareness and scope of death and the accessible grace of God in overcoming the vitality of death in this world that was stated, perhaps even understated, in the title *Instead of Death.*

The book was meant for adolescents and so it dwells upon a few of the issues—loneliness, sex, work—which adolescents must confront and through which the drama of death and resurrection is empirically verified. There was a pre-publication controversy about that also, since the premise of *Instead of Death* was that, if an adult tries to write to and for adolescents, the effort should be addressed to the problems of adolescents and not to those of adults or those which adults assume adolescents have. That premise was disputed particularly in connection with the chapter on "Sex and the Search for Self" because it rejects the customary notion that adolescents should be indoctrinated in the principles of "Christian marriage"—a theologically false idea anyway—or in marriage at all while they are of an age when marriage is generally not yet an option; at the same time it raises more immediate sexual questions concerning adolescents such as masturbation, homosexuality, and premarital sexual relations. Rereading that chapter recently, I thought it a bit quaint because of the supposed sexual liberation of everybody in the years since 1962. But if that chapter seems tame according to the current impressions about the sexual proclivities of the young, it only reinforces the premise just cited.

After vehement discussion, the manuscript was published as written, title and all, and the book has had an astonishing career. Probably more adults have read it than high school students; I constantly hear of its use in colleges; I continue to receive much correspondence prompted by it; and I have been made aware of its use by clergy for pastoral counseling.

I was glad, then, when The Seabury Press thought a revised and augmented edition of the book might now be appropriate. I reread the book to see how my views may have been influenced or altered by my experience since 1962. I am not fond of consistency, regarding it as a hobgoblin of the mind which tends to narrow and conform without good reason. Nevertheless, I found little in the original edition of *Instead of Death* that is inconsistent with my thought today. There are matters of nuance and emphasis, of scope and style, but there is nothing of substance that I would now wish to retract. That will surprise no one who has read any of my other books, most of them focusing upon the death/resurrection motif. If there is a trend to be detected in comparing the earlier with the later efforts, it is an increasing interest in the Bible.

I spend most of my life now with the Bible, reading or, more precisely, listening. My mundane involvements— practicing law, being attentive to the news of the moment, lecturing around the country, free lance pastoral counseling, writing, activity in church politics, maintaining my medical regime, doing chores around my home on Block Island—have become more and more intertwined with this major preoccupation of mine, so that I can no longer readily separate the one from the others. This merging for me of almost everything into a biblical scheme of living occurs because the data of the Bible and one's existence in common history is characteristically similar. One comes, after awhile, to live in a continuing biblical context and so is spared both an artificial compartmentalization of one's person and a false pietism in living.

The biblical adventure continues, I expect, for ever and ever; always familiar and always new, at once complete yet inexhaustible, both provocative and surprising, gratuitous and liberating. Insofar as I am a beneficiary of the biblical witness in the period between writing *Instead of Death* and now, the significant change which I am able to identify concerns the abolition of false dichotomies, as between the personal and the political or as between the private and the public. Thus, *Instead of Death* seeks to cope pastorally with a few issues which confront young people, as well as other persons, in self-conscious individual circumstances. But the theological connection of any of these matters to the ubiquity of the power of death and the redemptive vitality of the word of God in this world applies equally to political affairs and social crises and, moreover, does so in a way which renders apparently private concerns political.

Since *Instead of Death* was first written, this connection between the private and the political was verified to me by the illness which placed my life in crisis during the period from 1967 to 1969. A chronicle of that experience is related in *A Second Birthday* so I need not recapitulate the story here. It is enough to say that, through the danger of protracted illness, I realized that death—the death which so persistently threatened me, the death so aggressive in my body, the death signified by unremitting pain, the death which took the appearance of sickness—was familiar to me. I had encountered this same death elsewhere, in fact everywhere. The exposure to death of which I had total recall during the illness had occurred a decade or so earlier while I was working as a lawyer in East Harlem. In that urban ghetto my daily routine of cases and causes forced me to contend with death institutionalized in authorities, agencies, bureaucracies, and multifarious principalities and powers. Slowly I learned something which folk indigenous to the ghetto know: namely, that the power and purpose of death are incarnated in institutions and structures, procedures and regimes—Consolidated Edison or the Department of Welfare, the Mafia or the police, the Housing Authority or the social work bureaucracy, the hospital system or the banks, liberal philanthropy or corporate real estate speculation. In the wisdom of the people of the East Harlem neighborhood, such principalities are identified as demonic powers because of the relentless and ruthless dehumanization which they cause.

During my years in East Harlem, I became sufficiently enlightened about institutionalized death so that death was no longer an abstraction confined to the usual funereal connotations. I began then and there to comprehend death theologically as a militant, moral reality. The grandiose terms in which the Bible describes the power of death had begun to have a concrete significance for me. When, subsequently, death visited me in a most private and personalized manner, in the debilitations of prolonged illness and the aggressions of pain, I was able to recognize that this represented the same power—the same death—that I had before beheld in quite another guise, vested in the principalities active on the East Harlem scene. Unrelated as the two situations seemed to be, the one so public the other so private, there was an extraordinary and awful connection between the vitality and intent of death in each situation. The supposed dichotomy between the public and the personal appearance of death is both superficial and deceptive, enhancing the thrall of death over human beings.

This lack of distinction between the private and the political realms resolves a secret of the gospel which bothers and bemuses many churchpeople (though they seldom articulate their disturbance). Most churchfolk in American Christendom, especially those of a white, bourgeois background, have for generations, in both Sunday School and sanctuary, been furnished with an impression of Jesus as a person who went briefly about teaching love and doing good deeds: gentle Jesus, pure Jesus, meek Jesus, pastoral Jesus, honest Jesus, fragrant Jesus, passive Jesus, peaceful Jesus, healing Jesus, celibate Jesus, clean Jesus, virtuous Jesus, innocuous Jesus. Oddly enough, this image of Jesus is blatantly opposed to familiar biblical accounts of the ministry of Jesus. Those biblical accounts tell of a Jesus who was controversial in relation to his family and in synagogue appearances, who suffered poignantly, who suffered complete rejection by enemies and intimates alike, and who was greeted more often with apprehension than acclaim. This notion of an innocuous Jesus contradicts the notorious and turbulent events now marked as Holy Week in which Jesus is pursued as a political criminal by the authorities, put to trial and condemned, mocked and publicly humiliated, executed in the manner customarily reserved for insurrectionists, and, all the while, beheld by his followers with hysteria and consternation. While the traditional churches have invested so much in the innocuous image of Jesus, they have not been able to suppress the true events of Holy Week. This has placed churchpeople in the predicament of having two conflicting views of Jesus, not knowing whether the two are reconcilable and, if they are not, which one is to be believed. Most people probably never resolve the dilemma.

I recall how uneasy I used to feel when, as a young person in church during Lent and Holy Week, it suddenly seemed that all we had been told about Jesus during the other church seasons was being refuted by the gospel accounts. There were some obvious questions which would never even be mentioned, much less answered. Why, if Jesus was so private, so kind, so good, was he treated like a public criminal? Why would the state take any notice of him, much less crucify him? I realized that others noticed this discrepancy too. However, many people dealt with it merely by focusing on the image of an innocuous Jesus, overlooking the contradictory and disquieting evidence of Holy Week. Others chose a different way; they ideologized Jesus, rendering him a mere political agitator. I found both of these approaches deeply unsatisfactory; they were narrow and acculturated versions of Jesus, the one pietistic, the other political.

Even if the Church failed to deal with this discrepancy, one could still look to the New Testament to ascertain whether there was any basis for these contrasting images of Jesus and to try to comprehend the issues posed by Holy Week. I learned from the Bible that the answer to this problem involves the political significance of Jesus' works, discreet though they may have been, and the political implication of his sayings. Both his actions and sayings are cryptic: Jesus tells a parable ending with the remark "those who have ears, let them hear'' or he heals someone afflicted in mind or body and then cautions this person and any others who may have witnessed the event not to publicize it. It is only when the parables or his works become notorious (the precipitating episode being the raising of Lazarus) that the authorities move against Jesus. Why do these rulers regard Jesus with such apprehension? Why is he an offense and a threat to their regime? The answer that emerges in the biblical accounts is that, in teaching and healing, Jesus demonstrates an authority over the power of death. And it is that very same power of death which supplies the only moral sanction for the state and its ruling principalities.

Jesus preached and verified a freedom from the captivation of death which threatens the politics of this age in the most rudimentary way. Once they have learned of Jesus and of what he has said and done, the rulers accurately perceive this to be their undoing. Thus, the very events which have been most private or most discreet in Jesus' ministry take on the most momentous political meaning. And if the truth of this confrontation becomes public in the days of the Holy Week, it had been forecast throughout the life of Jesus— from Herod's attempt to murder the child, through the temptation to submit to the power of death (portrayed in explicit political terms) in the wilderness.

It is the power of death multifariously at work in the world which explains why the authorities cannot overlook the ministry of Jesus when it becomes apparent to them that he possessed authority and exercised a power over death, as exhibited in his preaching and healing. In the midst of the climactic public confrontation between the political principalities and Jesus during Holy Week (on Maundy Thursday) Jesus promised that his disciples would receive and share through his triumph over the power of death. And so it is that his promise is fulfilled at Pentecost. Thereafter, whenever that authority over death is shown—such as when Christians live faithfully in the power of the resurrection, freed from the captivation of intimidation of death—his people suffered and continue to suffer the hostility and harassment of the ruling principalities similar to that which Jesus had undergone.

The negation of the supposed distinction between the private and the political because of the coherence of death in diverse forms or appearances points to the truth that the resurrection, far from being the vague or ethereal immortality so commonly imagined, is eventful and accessible for human beings in every situation in which death is pervasive —in every personal or public circumstance in common history.

The message of the original *Instead of Death* is simply that the resurrection means the liberation of human life from the meaning and purpose of death in loneliness, in sexuality, and in daily work. These issues cannot be addressed pastorally with much competence, care, or common sense unless both their personal and political significance is recognized. My own experiences since *Instead of Death* was first written, particularly of illness, cause me to reiterate this all the more emphatically.

I am, therefore, persuaded not to tamper with the original manuscript in any extensive way. This book includes most of *Instead of Death* as it was first published. As I mentioned earlier, this was commissioned as a studybook for high school age youth. Thus questions were added to the original text for use by group leaders in discussion. Since none of that was my doing, it is here omitted. The omission signifies that this edition is not addressed self-consciously to any specific generation.

For that matter, even though I knew the earlier version was being published for circulation among teen-agers, I do not remember tailoring the manuscript for them except to the extent that the chapter on sexuality denounces "Christian marriage" as unbiblical, anti-sacramental, and irrelevant and also criticizes the use of this notion to suppress consideration of the more immediate existential sexual issues of youth. I have not altered that section here because the whole fantasy concerning "Christian marriage" remains a problem of the adult mentality, though many of the young today may have escaped it, at least insofar as they have become dropouts from so-called Christian education in the churches.

If some young people today are no longer importuned by misleading or false teaching about "Christian marriage" because they no longer attend church, others are extremely skeptical about marriage *per se* and especially about the morality of having children. The principality of the "American family" is challenged and questioned. I consider this a wholesome development specifically because this institution functions in order to achieve political, social, and economic conformity. My own commitment, vocationally, to celibacy has been informed to a great extent by concern for these demonic connotations of the American image of marriage and the family as the elemental institution of a white, middle class *status quo*.

Lately however, part of the disenchantment with marriage and the family has arisen due to the impact of technology upon sex. "The pill" is thought to supply liberation in sexual intercourse, freeing the parties from the risks of unwanted children. To such arguments I can only stress the theme which is basic to the discussion of sexuality in *Instead of Death:* that, essentially, freedom in sex involves

reverence for the personhood of the participants (this sym-
bolizing care for all persons) and *that* freedom originates in
the radical self-acceptance by which one is identified as a
person by the word of God. In that connection, technological developments affecting sex supply more temptation for
manipulation and abuse of persons (both of oneself and
others) than guarantees of liberation.

I believe the confusion attending the familiar and false
ideas about "Christian marriage" points to another issue
which has now become prominent. That is, of course, the
matter of sexism. This comes to the fore in the churches,
notably in the Episcopal and the Roman Catholic Churches,
in the controversy over the ordination of women to the
priesthood. My own involvement in the issue has been as
legal counsel to the women who have been ordained and
defense counsel to those priests who have suffered charges
in the ecclesiastical courts because they upheld the sacramental validity of these ordinations. I entertain no serious
doubt about the eventual outcome of this dispute, though it
is perhaps premature to state it. What has been ruefully
exposed is the depth, scope, and subtlety of sexism in the
Church: in the hierarchy, among clergy, and among both
male and female laity. It is marked, as racism so frequently
is, by people who remain curiously unaware of their own
condescension—condescension which could even be called
benignly motivated. This paternalistic sexism is motivated
by a need for status which necessitates the demeanment of
women. The pathetic dimension of the whole situation is
that, while there is no canonical impediment to the recognition of women as priests (on the contrary, there is a derelic-
tion of office where recognition is wrongfully withheld) and
while there is no respectable theological argument against
women in the priesthood, there has been an adamant refusal

to confront these women who have been ordained as human beings. The great uproar ensues as if these persons did not exist, as if they were not present. That signifies an appalling pastoral failure in the Episcopal Church, specifically involving many incumbent bishops. It is a dysfunction which has occasioned the collapse of more than one bishop into hysteria. In other words, as with racism, sexism becomes conspicuous not only in the oppression and humiliation of its victims, but also in the dehumanization and anxiety of its practitioners. Thus, ironically, the cause of the victim becomes an intercession for the plight of the oppressor, even as in the historical ministry of Jesus Christ.

In any case, the various questions pertaining to sexuality (to sexual roles and relationships) for women and for men, for adolescents and for adults, cannot be sorted out without reference to the gospel or, for that matter, without first dealing with the more rudimentary reality of sexism in this culture.

How convoluted sexism really is, how far the churches echo the culture, has also been disclosed in the emergence of congregations largely composed of homosexuals who are confessing Christians, and in connection with the question of ordaining acknowledged homosexuals. As to the latter, it seems relevant that many homosexuals have been and are being ordained, though without the candor that some are now insisting upon. I welcome any opportunity to dispense with hypocrisy in the churches. As to the homosexually-oriented sects that have arisen, the chief concern is that they are *sects*, congregations separated from the rest of the Church largely on the basis of specific identification; in this case homophilia, though it could be anything else—a particular gift, race, tongue or language, nationality, profession, class, age, or singular belief. Any sect detracts from the ecumenical integrity to which the Church is called in the gospel. Thus it is the world which is characteristically broken and divided. The Church must not conform to such fragmentation but be the image of reconciled humanity in society. Any sect, therefore, is primarily a sign of apostasy and wordliness within the Church. For that reason I regret the homophile sects. But the appropriate response to them is not denunciation or rejection but, rather, the renewal of the ecumenical reality of the Church so that there is no need for such sects.

And to those who still indulge hackneyed exigesis which dwells upon scattered texts to argue that the Bible consigns homosexuals to damnation, I think it only necessary to mention that by the same misleading interpretation the Bible so consigns the gluttons and the rich, merchants and warmakers, and, indeed, all the rulers of the world. If such sanctions were honored, the churches of America would suddenly be drastically depleted.

As to the remaining sections of *Instead of Death* represented here, the essay on loneliness was first written on the day I had news of the suicide of a friend. In the circumstance, I was preoccupied with loneliness as it afflicts the young. As I have since become more proximate to the old, I see that the dread of loneliness returns poignantly; that furthers a conviction that, in this society, the young and the old have the most in common since they are treated so similarly—both suffering a sub-human status, the one inhibited, the other discarded.

The chapter on work, in this revision, becomes indispensable to the theological comprehension of the new material dealing with the consumption ethic and the impact of technology on politics, since both of the latter extend the biblical definition of work (the radical estrangement between human life and the rest of creation) to the realm of institutional powers and ruling authorities.

The closing section is, as in the original version, a look at how the event of becoming a Christian relates to the gift for coping with the militancy and versatility of the power of death.

William Stringfellow
BLOCK ISLAND, RHODE ISLAND
The day of the beheading of John the Baptist, 1975

I.

The Presence and Power of Death

> For as by a man came death, by a man has
> come also the resurrection of the dead. For as
> in Adam all die, so also in Christ shall all be
> made alive.
>
> *I Corinthians 15:21–22*

This is a book about death.

It consists of essays about the concrete reality of death in contemporary life; about the vitality of the presence and power of death over human existence and, indeed, over the whole of creation. The suggestion here is that the power of death can be identified in American society—as well as elsewhere for that matter—as the pervasive, decisive, reigning, ultimate power. Therefore, for an individual's own small life—yours or mine or anybody's—death is the reality that has the most immediate, personal, everyday significance. In this life, it seems that everyone and everything finds meaning in death.

No ambition is expressed here to treat the presence and activity of death exhaustively, but only to deal with it suggestively. That is, to say enough to provoke some further thought and consideration of the matter; to suggest only enough to convince a reader that it is not possible to be a human being very long without coming to terms in one way or another with the presence of death in one's own life and in the relationship between one's own life and the lives of all other people and things.

SIGNS OF DEATH IN URBAN LIFE

The particular focus here is upon the signs of death and evidences of the activity of death in American urban culture, especially as they affect a person in daily life and work. That focus is chosen, for one thing, because the city is my own habitat; it is the place I know. But also the city represents some sort of fruition of American society; more precisely, the city represents some sort of terminal point of American society. Be that as it may, the city increasingly dominates the whole of American life, just as colonialism did earlier and the frontier did later on. No one escapes involvement—politically, economically, culturally, psychologically, personally—with the city, whether he recognizes it and likes it or not.

Today the city is the place where all the forces, purposes, powers, and factors dispersed throughout society have converged and been brought into radical, complex, and delicate juxtaposition with one another. You do not escape the issues of modern American urban life by living in Bangor, San Jose, or a farm in Iowa; and you certainly do not mitigate them by moving out of New York to Darien or Scarsdale. You cannot even hide from the same issues in Magnolia, Mississippi. The issues of urban life permeate the whole society and culture of the United States, and the question is not whether they can be avoided or whether you can somehow hide from them, but how you or I or anyone else can come to terms with them and confront them with intelligence and frankness.

Moreover, you need not live in Manhattan or Detroit rather than Evanston or Amherst to recognize the common problems of human life. In the slums and in the suburbs, among both poor and rich, black and white, the elderly and the young, men and women, the literate and the illiterate, the lives of people encompass buying and selling, fighting and forgiving, working and playing, illness and health, hate and love—living for awhile in all these ways and then dying and, after a time, being forgotten. The significant issues of life are essentially the same for every person in every place as they are for you or me.

Although these issues are present and as serious outside the city as within the city, they are more obvious and open in the city; perhaps more exaggerated, more dramatized there. Certainly in the city they are evident in a magnitude, scope, and concentration that makes it impossible to ignore them or to pretend that they are not there. Hence, by looking at the city, one glimpses the whole American scene so far as the ordinary human issues are concerned.

Remembering that this book is to be suggestive, not exhaustive, provocative, not definitive, attention is concentrated only on certain issues that mark the life of a person, particularly a young person, in today's urban culture. These issues—seen here as signs of the power of death at work in American society—are loneliness, sex, and the search for personal identity, work, leisure, and security.

Such issues cannot, of course, be neatly isolated from each other or from a host of other issues which might also be raised. The underlying thought in this book is that they are most profoundly related by that to which each of them is a witness in the common experience of people—*death*. Death, in other words, is what all men truly have in common with each other and with the whole of creation. Death is what you have in common with me and the only reality, it seems, that we have in common with everyone else and everything else in this world.

DEATH, EVIL, AND SIN

Do not confuse death with either evil or sin, as is so often done in careless teaching and preaching in the churches. Death is to be carefully distinguished from both evil and sin. Each is related to the other, but they are different realities. For one thing, death is not the consequence of either evil or sin, nor is death some punishment for evil or sin. Nor is there any such thing as objective evil; that is, some knowledge or idea or principle of evil which people can learn or discover or discern and then, by their own will, do evil or good. If humans knew or could know what is good and what is evil in that sense, then they would be like God himself.

But people are just human—not like God. Evil, in the sense in which men know of evil, exists only in some action, word, deed, or other event that threatens the self-interest (not, notice, selfish interest, but self-interest, that is, welfare) of a person, institution, ideology, or nation. Yet that which seems to be evil from the vantage point of one invariably turns out to be good for another. The terms *good* and *evil* in this sense, and except when they are used to refer to the action of God in judging the world, have meaning relative to the self-interest of a person or country or whatever; they are not ultimate or abstract terms. What you or I might, in any given situation, think to be evil is always a very ambiguous, uncertain, and partial insight, because what you or I can see of the situation—much less foresee of the consequences of the situation—is limited, prejudiced, and identified with our own interest in our own lives and with the consequences that seem to affect our own lives.

That is why, in part, what one person or nation considers to be good or evil can *never* be claimed by that person or nation to be the equivalent or even the approximation of God's judgment, although persons and nations constantly make just that pretense. They do it as a way of mocking God, as a way of pretending that they can second guess how God will judge their decisions or actions, as a way of asserting that they already know how God will judge themselves and others. That is perilous because only a person *who does not believe in God* would so seriously usurp and absurdly challenge the freedom of God in judging all persons and all things in all the world. That is an arrogant and a dangerous course because it is a way of playing God.

Indeed it is just this pretension to know beforehand how God judges and will judge human decisions and actions that is the essence of sin. Sin is not essentially the mistaken, inadvertent, or deliberate choice of evil by human beings, but the pride into which they fall in associating their own self-interests with the will of God. Sin is the denunciation of the freedom of God to judge humans as it pleases him to judge them. Sin is the displacement of God's will with one's own will. Sin is the radical confusion as to whether God or the human being is morally sovereign in history. And those persons who suppose that *they* are sovereign exist in acute estrangement in this history, separated from life itself and from the giver of life, from God. In that state, alienated from all of life, including their own life and the life of all others and all things, they are consigned to death, committed to the service of death, unable to save themselves from death.

Death is not the same reality as evil, but there is evil in death. That which is evil in death is the threat that death embodies of lost identity, of obliteration, of extinction, of the ruthless and final negation of self. There is evil in death, in this sense, because death is adverse to the most profound and elementary self-interest of a person or a society—the mere preservation of life.

DEATH AND YOUTH

To some, I suppose, it may seem vulgar or irrelevant or otherwise inappropriate to write candidly about death. The custom in America is not to mention death—even at funerals. And least of all is death openly mentioned among or in front of the young, except when it is mentioned during their baptisms. Yet death does not wait for full maturity and adulthood, for infirmity or age, for sickness or weakness to assail human life. The work of death begins at the very moment of birth: death claims every person in the first consciousness of existence. Death does not respect or wait upon the foolish amenities which cause people to hide from their offspring the truth that, for all the ingenuity and capability of human beings, death is present, powerful, and active in every moment, in every event and transaction of human experience.

No one is given birth who does not imminently confront the claim of death over his own life.

IS DEATH THE LAST WORD?

Ironically, though death is seldom frankly discussed and though the meaning of death is clothed in superstition and myth, an underlying preoccupation with death is evident everywhere. The fear of death, especially the fear of one's own death, though sublimated, is the most universal dread men suffer.

The law, for example, is very much concerned with death, for the ultimate sanction of the law is the power of the state to take life—and all the lesser penalties exacted by the law are symbols of this final sanction.

On the other hand, many people are fascinated and entertained by those in the performing arts and sports who risk their lives, matching their own courage and skill against death, as circus performers, bullfighters, or auto stunt drivers do. In literature and the other creative arts, a recurrent theme is death and the probing of the meaning of death in this life. Even in those corny and seemingly ridiculous old horror films like *Frankenstein* the issue is the presence and power of death in this world and the attempt—the unsane, sometimes insane, always futile attempt—of humans to overcome the power of death.

Death is very much on the minds of people, and the mystery of death is given much attention, despite the conventional folkways in America that ban the mention of it in plain or personal language.

Do not laugh or scoff at the venerable images of the power of death named the "Devil" or the "Angel of Death," for they are ways in which men have recognized that death is a living, active, decisive reality. And that is indeed what death is, how ever the face of death is visualized or portrayed. Such images of death are far more realistic than the modern superstitions that seek to avoid or altogether deny the vitality of death in daily life. Such images are wiser than the mythology associated with the meaning of death that treats death as if it were merely some destination; that is, as if death were abstract and remote from today and every day, a reality only to be faced eventually, on some distant terminal day. Such images are more discerning than the now popular idea that death simply means biological extinction.

Death is all that and more. Death is the contemporaneous power abrasively addressing every person in one's own existence with the word that one is not only eventually and finally, but even now and already, estranged, separated, alienated, lost in relationships with everybody and everything else, and—what is in a way much worse—one's very own self. Death means a total loss of identity.

Death, in *this* sense—death embodying this awful threat —is the death which is at work not only on the day of the undertaker, but today.

This is a book about death. It is, as well, a book about resurrection.

Of all the worldly powers, death is the most obvious, but death is not the greatest power active in the world. Death is not the last word. Nor is the last word some nebulous, fanciful, fake promise of an after life. If you have been told or taught anything such as that in church, what you have heard is heresy. The last word is not death, nor life after death; the last word is the same as the first word, and *that* word is Jesus Christ. He has, holds, and exercises power even over death in this world. And his promise is that a person may be set free from bondage to death in this life here and now.

II.

Loneliness, Dread, and Holiness

> Three times I besought the Lord about this,
> that it should leave me; but he said to me,
> "My grace is sufficient for you, for my power
> is made perfect in weakness. . ."
>
> *II Corinthians 12:8–9*

Loneliness is as intimate and as common to human beings as death.

Loneliness does not respect persons, but afflicts all—men and women, those of status and the derelicts, the adolescents and the old people, the single and the married, the learned and the illiterate, and, one might add, the clergy and the laity.

It is an ordinary affliction, though perhaps more noticed

and more readily admitted among some than others—
among those, for instance, whose loneliness becomes so
desperate as to be pathological, or among those forgotten
by society in prisons or hospitals or boweries, or among
both older and younger single folk.

Loneliness is more evident in the city, or so it seems,
since the largest group of people now migrating to the city
are no longer distinguished by nationality or race but by the
fact that they are single. These migrants are mainly young
people—students or recent graduates, artists and professionals, white-collar workers of all sorts—coming to the city to
work and live and look for each other. Taken with the older
people of the city—the widowed and the retired—they
make single people a very substantial part of the urban
population.

That the proportion of young single people in the city is
greater than elsewhere does not prove that loneliness is any
more prevalent in the city, but it is perhaps more apparent
in the city. The fictions that attach to the escape from
loneliness are perchance pursued and practiced more publicly and more frantically in the city. The very size of the
city, not to mention the variety and versatility of the city's
life, promises at best some therapy for loneliness and at
least some distraction from it.

Loneliness is the specific apprehension of a person of his
or her own death in relation to the impending death of all
persons and all things. Loneliness is the experience in
which the fear of one's own personal death coincides with
one's fright of the death of everyone and everything else.
Loneliness is not a unique or an isolated experience; on the
contrary, it is the ordinary but still overwhelming anxiety
that all relationships are lost. Loneliness does not deny or
negate the existence of lives other than the life of the one
who is lonely, but loneliness so vividly anticipates the death

of such other lives that they are of no sustenance or comfort to the life and being of the one who suffers loneliness.

Loneliness is the most caustic, drastic, and fundamental repudiation of God. Loneliness is the most elementary expression of original sin. There is no one who does not know loneliness. Yet there is no one who is alone.

FICTIONS OF LONELINESS

This subject is so profoundly subjective that one cannot even pretend to be analytical about it. However, some of the fictions associated with loneliness can be identified, even though they cannot be sharply distinguished.

. . . .*that it is unfilled time*

One fiction is that loneliness is contingent upon time; that loneliness essentially means unfilled or unused time. Loneliness is thought to be a vacuum in which one exists between periods of occupation in work or play, or in the absence of companions. Loneliness, here, is the experience of void.

Many persons just work to death, at first in school activities, either studies or extracurricular work, and later in a job. They leave school or the job only to sleep alone or eat alone, and they try to remain so occupied and preoccupied in their work that the empty time is filled.

The void may be filled by activities which merely use up surplus time because of a shortage of school activities or other work or play or companionship. The exploitation of boredom in the city, the supply of things to do and places to go in order just to spend leftover time, is organized commercially in an elaborate fashion. Dance studios catering to both young and old, health salons and gyms, clubs engaged in acquainting people with each other, private parties to which invitations can be purchased, sometimes church youth groups—all of these, and many more, traffic in boredom and profit in one way or another from promising that time will be consumed for those who pay the price.

Some people, young as well as old, never get around to spending their boredom in the presence of others, but spend it physically alone gazing at whatever happens to appear on their television set or entranced with the noise of a transistor radio. It is as if the sight or sound of other human beings, without any direct or serious involvement with them, were enough to prove that they are not alone.

On every corner of the city is a bar—not the elegant places which cater to the transient lonely, but the little, cruddy neighborhood taverns, the kind that can also be found in almost any small town. Bars in which, night after night, the very same people who live side by side in the same block or building sit side by side on rows of stools exchanging boredom for oblivion.

For those as yet not old enough or old enough looking to drink, there is a hangout on the corner—a candy store or soda fountain or hamburger joint—where one can find some privacy from parents and teachers (if not from cops) and get lost in the noise of the music or in the anonymity of a gang.

You can, of course, patronize more esoteric establishments with special clienteles—prostitutes or homosexuals or gamblers or whatever one wants—and there relieve loneliness in lust and chance.

. . . .that it can be satisfied in erotic infatuation

These are places often frequented by those who realize that loneliness is more than the burden of time and who are beguiled by another fiction—that loneliness is satisfied in erotic infatuation. Here are people—men or women, boys or girls—looking for the same or the other sex; people for whom seduction finally becomes a way of life. Here are people insisting upon the importance of what meets the eye or other senses: external impressions, physique, cosmetics, the appearances of youth.

Here are the lonely whose search for some partner is so dangerous, so stimulating, and so exhausting that the search itself provides an apparent escape from loneliness. But when the searching stops, when a partner is found for an hour or a night or an affair, the search immediately resumes. The searching becomes compulsive. And while erotic companionship seems more appealing and more human than resignation to boredom, while touching each other may be more intimate and more honest than watching each other, no one can really overcome his loneliness or find his own identity in another, least of all in the body of another.

. . . .*that it can be answered in possession*

Perhaps that is the most absurd fiction of them all: the primitive notion present in erotic partnerships—*but also very often in other relationships, between parents and children, in friendship, in marriage*—that the answer to loneliness, that one's own identity, must be sought and is to be found in another person. This is, of course, an idea of venerable origin; the early Greeks thought men and women were two halves in pursuit of a whole person to be found in their union. It is also an idea of contemporary popularity. Think of the ridiculous idealism of much instruction about "Christian marriage" or think of the erotica disguised and presented on television and through other mass media.

To pursue and take one's own identity from the person

of another is to equate love with possession. Fits of jealousy are inevitable in any such liaison, for each time the other's attention or affection is drawn to somebody else, the one whose identity is taken from that other's life is damaged. At worst the fiction that one's identity is to be found in another is cannibalistic—a devouring of another; at best it is a possessive, if romantic, manipulation of one by another in the name of love.

LONELINESS AS A FORETASTE OF DEATH

None of these fictions significantly addresses the experience of loneliness; none is more than an illusory comfort for the lonely. Separately or together they are omens of the very reality of which loneliness is the foretaste: *death*. How then could any of them have power to answer loneliness? How could any do other than dramatize loneliness all the more? Is there any answer to loneliness?

Will you look for release in your work? It can fill the time but not the void. Work is the estrangement of men from the rest of creation. Work—as it is discussed later in this book—means the bondage of human beings to the rest of creation, a sign of death, as great a burden to humans as the isolation of persons from each other which is time.

Will you turn then to leisure? Leisure is merely another word for work, embodying the same animosity between men and the rest of creation. Leisure, or non-work in any of its other forms, is as much an anticipation of death as work.

Perhaps another drink will help. Maybe a drink will induce you to forget that this loneliness is not the absence of others, but your presence among others when your presence is treated as absence. Perhaps another drink will help you to forget that you are regarded as if you are dead. Perhaps another drink will let you forget you are forgotten.

Get some sex. If you find some, maybe you will find yourself too. If you find some, at least you will not be alone, though you will still be lonely. And if, after awhile, you have no luck in finding either sex or yourself, your fatigue in the search will overcome both your desire and your need, and then, at least, you will be able to sleep alone again long enough to wake refreshed to resume the search. Live in the consolation of looking for what you need where it surely cannot be found and you will always harbor, if nothing else, a little false hope. That is the way to die.

See a psychiatrist. You cannot cope with loneliness alone. Maybe, if you search yourself and your biography with a doctor's patience, you can find something or someone to blame yourself upon. Anyway, you can explain your anxieties to him, even if he cannot absolve you of any guilt. Perhaps he can help you to abide your own death, even though he cannot save you from it.

Maybe you will find a lover. Any face that passes on the street might be your lover. Do you wonder how you look to those who pass? Do they wonder the same of you? Dare you speak? Or make any gesture? If you do, they may turn away. They may murder you when all you want is their love. No. Loneliness is more familiar than annihilation, and thus seems more secure. Better stay where you are.

Try marriage. It is the more sensible course. You ought to be able to make a go of it. Lots have. No more returning to an empty room; there will be another to share the emptiness. And, who knows? There may be more to share than that. Your better half may be the part of you that's missing. You may discover who you are in your mate, or, failing that, in your offspring; that would be better than dying as you are, alone.

Be more positive! Now there's a thought. Defeat your loneliness by affirming that it does not exist. Hypnotize yourself. Make believe, as children do, and it will seem, for a little while, just as you pretend, until, of course, the rueful day when you realize that things are not as bad as they seem only because, in fact, they seem as bad as they are.

End it now. This living is not life. It is death. Why not salute the fact and dramatize it? Wherever you turn you see the face of death: all these disguises do not hide *that* face. All these temptations are emissaries of death. The presence of death is hidden everywhere, the power of death is awful. Why not find out how great death is? End it all now. If death is so great then this foretaste of death, this loneliness, will be ended in death, too. Then you won't be lonely anymore. Then you won't be.

Poor you! Pity yourself—everybody else does. Loathe the fact that you cannot remember who you are and so no one else can recognize you. Hate—hate is a form of pity—the fact that you are someone other than the one you wish to be, other than the one you imagine would earn the love of others. (Love cannot be earned. No one deserves a gift, else where's the act of giving? Love is volunteered, and if you do not know that you are loved, it is not you who are rejected, it is you who are repudiating the one who loves you. Pity yourself for that.)

Pray. It is a last resort, I know. Still, nothing else dispels this gruesome desolation. But how do you do it? That's just the trouble. Prayer is nothing you do, prayer is someone you are. Prayer is not about doing, but being. Prayer is about being alone in God's presence. Prayer is being *so* alone that God is the only witness to your existence. The secret of prayer is God affirming your life. To be *that* alone is incompatible with loneliness. In prayer you cannot be lonely. It *is* the last resort.

THE SURRENDER TO DEATH AND THE TRIUMPH OF GRACE

There is no person who does not know loneliness—even Jesus Christ knew it. He did not succumb to loneliness because there is no person who is alone.

On the face of the Gospel narrative is the lonely Christ. Nobody greeted, nobody honored, nobody understood, nobody loved, nobody celebrated his vocation. Nobody loved him for being the one he is.

In his birth he was sought as an earthly ruler. He suffered the rebuke of Mary and Joseph when, as a child, he was found in the Temple in discourse with the teachers. When he submitted to baptism, he bewildered a protesting John the Baptist. It was rejection he experienced when his relatives called on him to name them in preference to the crowd. He healed the sick, but both sick and well mistook his power. When he spoke in the Temple, he was not heard or heeded. The same temptations that visited him in the wilderness returned to taunt him in the political triumph of Palm Sunday, and his own disciples were—and many are to this very day—astonished and perplexed that he withstood such attractive temptations. Israel, which had boasted in her waiting for his coming, found him subversive when he came. Rome was an accomplice in his condemnation. At Gethsemane, while he was alone in prayer, his friends slept and his enemies plotted to destroy him. Judas betrayed him, Peter denied him, all the rest fled. A thief ridiculed him on the Cross. The people shouted for his death.

Unwelcome, misunderstood, despised, rejected, unloved and misloved, condemned, betrayed, deserted, helpless— he was delivered to death as if he were alone.

Christ descended into hell; Christ is risen from death.

In the submission of Christ to death, the power of death is dissipated. In the subjection of Christ to death, the dread is taken out of loneliness. Christ suffered loneliness without despair. In the radical loneliness of Christ is the assurance that no one is alone.

In surrender to death, in hell, in the event in which the presence and power of death is most notorious, undisguised, militant, and pervasive, the reality and grace of God are triumphant.

In the event in which you are alone with your own death

—when all others and all things are absent and gone—God's initiative affirms your very creation and that you are given your life anew. In the moment and place where God is least expected—in the barrenness and emptiness of death—God is at hand. It is in that event that a person discovers it is death which is alone, not he.

LONELINESS AND THE ETHICS OF HOLINESS

There is no one who does not know loneliness; not even Jesus Christ. But Christ himself has shown that there is no one who is alone.

You are not alone. Do not be so proud any more of your loneliness. It is only the shadow of your death; and your death, your loneliness, is like the death of every other man. But your death is overpowered in the patience of God's love for you. Your fear that you are not loved does not negate the gift which God's love is. Your loneliness does not avoid God's love, it only repudiates his love for you. You cannot flee from God's presence. You are not alone.

Now you are free. You are free from the idol your own death becomes in loneliness. You are free from all the frantic escapes, free from trying to purchase love, free from anonymity. You are free now from searching, because you have been found. You are free. Your life is found in the life of God. You are not alone.

Now you can love. Love yourself. That is the rudiment of all other loves. Love yourself: that means your final acceptance of and active participation in God's love of you. Love yourself. If you love yourself you will become and be one who can love another. Love yourself and then your love of others will be neither suicidal nor destructive, neither jealous nor possessive; but then your love of yourself will enable, embody, enrich, and elucidate your love of others, and your other loves will do the same to your self-love. And when you love others, tell them so. Celebrate it—not only by some words but by your life toward them and toward the whole of the world. Your specific love of another is verified and supported in your love of all others and all things, even those or that which seem to be unlovable, which seem unworthy to be loved. Let that be the manner of your witness to the one who loves although none are worthy, not even one. You are not alone.

Don't be afraid. There is no more to fear. Do not fear rejection. If you fear rejection by another you do not love the other, though you may profess it. You are only being anxious for his love of you. The free man does not seek the love of others, nor fear that his love will be rejected, for rejection—as is known from the night in which Christ was betrayed—does not destroy love, and it does not destroy the one who loves. Don't be afraid, you are not alone.

Now you are whole. Your work and the time you spend not working now both become sacraments of the solidarity between yourself and the rest of creation, sacraments of the reconciliation wrought, for you, by Christ. Now work and leisure become virtually indistinguishable from worship, that is, from the enjoyment of God's love not just for you, but for all, including those who do not yet enjoy God's love for themselves or for anyone or anything else.

The enjoyment of God in this way is, of course, the estate of holiness. Holiness does not mean that you are any better than anyone else; holiness is not the same as goodness; holiness is not common piety. Holiness is not about pleasing God, even less about appeasing God. Holiness is about enjoying God. Holiness is the integrity of greeting, confessing, honoring, and trusting God's presence in all events and in any event, no matter what, no matter when, no matter where.

Therefore, rejoice. Reckon your weakness as praise of God's power. Endure suffering in joy. Risk your life on the veracity of Christ. Count your loneliness a means of grace.

III.

Sex and The Search for Self

Now concerning the unmarried, I have no command of the Lord, but I give my opinion as one who by the Lord's mercy is trustworthy.

I Corinthians 7:25

In sex, whatever the species or practice, the issue is not pleasure or lust, but personal identity.

Sex is by no means the only way in which the quest for personal identity is pursued. It may be sought in daily work, in the upbringing of children, in that for which one spends money, in sports, in study, or in the practice of the arts. Whatever the case in these other realms, the search for self is the most characteristic aspect of sex.

The discovery of self, or, more precisely, the recovery of self—the gift of personal identity—is, at the same time, the very theme of the gospel. Christ is, pre-eminently, the one who knows what it is to be a human being. Christ is the true image of humanity amidst a people who do not know what it is to be fully human; amidst those, including his own family and his disciples, who are profoundly troubled about their own identities and both wondrously attracted to and pathetically threatened by his presence. They do not know who they are as persons for the very reason that they have not yet recognized who he is.

It is impossible to consider sex seriously in terms of the search for self without eventually confronting the promise of the gospel that the secret of personal identity for *every* person is found in Christ. It is just this—what it means to be human—that is the essential content of what the gospel affirms about sex. It is this and not the conventional denunciations, heard in so many churches, of sex as sin or of sex as something foul or dirty or animalistic. It is this and not surrender to the temptation to suppress sex and the subject of sex in the churches or, what is worse, the more common temptation to condone sex as long as it is discreetly practiced—condemning it only when it becomes a matter of scandal.

In other words, it is quite all right to mention sex in the sanctuary, just as it is also appropriate to speak within the Church of any other matter that occupies the attentions of people in the world. The life and action within the sanctuary has integrity only insofar as it is concerned with and encompasses the life that takes place outside the sanctuary. Nothing that has ever been done in a bedroom, in the back seat of a car, or, for that matter, in a brothel is beyond the scope of the gospel and, therefore, beyond the Church's care for the world. The fantasies, fears, and fairy tales associated with sex must be dispelled so that, within the Church, sex is admitted, discussed, and understood with intelligence, maturity, compassion, and, most of all, a reverence for the ministry of Christ in restoring human life to human beings.

SEX AND THE SANCTUARY

In the churches and especially among youth, sex is treated as if it does not seriously exist or as if it ought not seriously to exist before or outside of marriage. Thus the Church generally sublimates or ignores the fact that sex is a profoundly influential reality in the daily lives of young people. Too often, young people at church youth conferences and Sunday Schools must sit through presentations about "marriage and the family" that offer only simplified, idealized, foolish, and often false images of sex, and which treat sex as an obligation exclusive to marriage and procreation. At the same time, these presentations shun the immediate sexual issues confronting young people who, according to the realities of modern American life, are practically—that is, economically and educationally, if not psychologically and physiologically—unable to marry for many more years (after school or college, after military service, after landing a job, after saving some money, after a long while).

Meanwhile, the immediate sexual problems and questions that commonly assail young people are more often than not neglected, unmentioned, and even considered unmentionable. In effect, the existence of petting and fondling, premarital and extramarital intercourse, masturbation, homosexuality, sexual adjustment in relationships with parents and teachers and other adults, and the mystery of sex and love are denied.

[39]

To confront young people with an ideal of "Christian marriage" that is beyond the possibility of prompt, practical fulfillment for them does not contribute to the nurture of these adolescents, nor does it enhance the prospects of a mature and stable adulthood.

Furthermore, it would be more healthy, human, and honest for churchpeople—instead of dwelling so exclusively on the image of marriage—to distinguish the varieties of sexual experimentation and sex acts on the one hand, and the fact of sexuality on the other, and then admit to themselves and to youth that *all* relationships are, in some sense and to some degree, sexual; relationships between a husband and wife, of course, but also between parent and child, friend and friend, one and another wherever they meet, whatever their gender. Sexuality is an aspect of every human transaction or communication, though nothing may happen to dramatize the fact, and though in any relationship it is *never* the sole reality. The sexuality of all persons should make us aware of just how common sexual activity is; how familiar it is in one way or another to everybody and how, therefore, it is a matter which cannot ever be effectively ignored or suppressed. (Indeed the suppression of sex, the refusal or fear of discussing the realities of sex, the denial of the ordinary sexuality of persons, are all sexual acts, though they may be somewhat preverse ones.) Sexuality is universal. Sex is mundane. That is reason enough for sex to be dealt with candidly and realistically within the Church.

THE NOTION OF CHRISTIAN MARRIAGE

There really is no such thing as "Christian marriage" as the term is commonly used. "Christian marriage" is a vain, romantic, unbiblical conception. "Christian marriage" is a fiction. There is no more an institution of "Christian marriage" than there is a "Christian nation" or a "Christian lawyer" or a "Christian athlete." Even where such terms are invoked as a matter of careless formulation and imprecise speech, they are symptoms of a desire to separate Christians from the common life of the world, whereas Christians are called into radical involvement in the common life of the world. To be sure, there are Christians who are athletes and those who practice law, and there are Christians who are citizens of this and the other nations. But none of these or similar activities or institutions are in any respect essentially Christian, nor can they be changed or reconstituted in order to become Christian. They are, on the contrary, realities of the fallen life of the world. They are inherently secular and worldly; they are subject to the power of death; they are aspects of the present, transient, perishing existence of the world.

It is the same with marriage. Marriage is a fallen estate. That does not mean that it is not an honorable estate, but only that it is a relationship subject to death. It is a relationship established in and appropriate for the present age, but not known or, more precisely, radically transcended and transfigured in both the Creation and the Eschaton—in both the beginning and the end of human history.

As with any other reality of secular life, the Christian takes marriage seriously for what it is, but for no more or less than that. The Christian does not suffer illusions about marriage, but recognizes that marriage is a civil contract in which two parties promise to exchange certain services and responsibilities with respect to each other and to assume certain obligations for offspring of the marriage. At the same time, marriage is no merely private contract, for society at large has a particular interest in the honoring and enforcement of this contract. If the marriage contract is observed and performed with reasonable diligence, society, as well as the married couple and their children, benefits since an enduring marriage contributes to the economic, social, and psychological stability of the whole of society.

The fiction that there is some ideal of marriage for Christians which is better than or essentially different from an ordinary secular marriage is not only fostered by most Sunday School curriculum materials on the subject, but also by the practice of authorizing the clergy to act for the state in the execution of the marriage contract. Clergymen are licensed by the state to perform the functions of a civil magistrate, in spite of the supposed separation of church and state in this country. This both lends weight to the confusion about "Christian marriage," and greatly compromises the discretion of the clergy as to whom they shall marry. In the office and function of a civil magistrate, no clergyman really has the grounds to refuse to marry any two people who present themselves to him, whether they are Christians or not, whether they are temperamentally or otherwise ready to marry, as long as they meet the civil requirements for marriage; that is, are of a certain age, have had blood tests, meet any residence requirements, have a valid license, and pay the fee.

A more theologically responsible practice, I suggest, would be to divest the clergy of this civil office and require that all who will be married present themselves to the civil magistrate to be married. Then, if those who are so married are Christians, they will go to their congregation to offer, within the company of the Church, their marriage to be blessed, to seek the intercessions of the whole Church for the marriage, and to celebrate their marriage in the Church as a sacrament. A similar practice is followed in many parts of Europe and Latin America.

To restore such a practice would go a long way toward recovering the sacramental integrity of marriage between Christians. For to discard the fiction of "Christian marriage" and to understand that marriage is an ordinary, secular, and fallen estate in no way denigrates marriage for Christians. On the contrary, in marriage and all else the Christian is fully participant in secular life; but at the same time he is constantly engaged in offering his involvement in secular life for the glory of God. In such an offering, that which is ordinary is rendered extraordinary, that which is merely worldly is transfigured, that which is most common becomes the means of worship, and each act or event of everyday life becomes sacramental—a sign and celebration of God's care for every act and event of everyday life in this world. Rather than demean or downgrade marriage, to restore such a practice would again give to the marriages of Christians the dignity of that which is secular made holy, of that which is a sign of death become a witness to redemption to all those, married or not, who are not Christian.

SEX AND SOCIETY

The confusion about the meaning of marriage is very modest compared to that associated with sexual acts or experiences prior to or outside of marriage such as premarital and extramarital intercourse, masturbation, petting, homosexuality, and so on, though these are matters of more immediate and constant concern to most young people. The churches have treated these matters too occasionally, too superficially, and too pietistically.

It is of first importance to acknowledge that no person is the judge of any other, nor is a person even his or her own judge, nor is society the judge, nor, least of all, is the Church the judge of anyone. Each and every human being, this society and all societies, the Church and the churches—all are judged in the event of the Word of God and in no other way.

Society is not the judge, but society does seek to preserve itself. For the sake of self-preservation, society—through law or custom—condones conduct that is deemed socially beneficial and condemns conduct that is deemed detrimental to the peace and welfare of society. But, as the Church of England has authoritatively recognized, what society considers from time to time to be criminal or otherwise antisocial behavior is not synonymous with sin.

Society generally condemns sexual acts involving coercion, public nuisance, or breach of the peace as criminally antisocial. However, under the impact of the more recent insights of psychiatry and psychology, the law tends to consider acts such as these as symptomatic of illness rather than of criminal intent and therefore more appropriately treated by medicine than by confinement in prison.

In some cases, sexual acts may not violate any criminal statutes or even be justifiably classified as criminal. But, nonetheless, they constitute antisocial behavior and therefore suffer the moral censure of society. This is so, for example, where conduct tends to undermine the integrity, stability, and performance of the marriage contract, as in the case of extramarital intercourse and perhaps most, but not necessarily all, incidents of premarital intercourse; in incestuous relations between parents and children—which are, incidentally, far more common than is generally conceded; and in some homosexual liaisons, like those where one of the partners is married.

Obviously, certain forms of sexual behavior are not intrinsically antisocial, although some particular sexual act in a specific instance may represent a form of personal hostility toward society, nonconformity, maladjustment to society, or simply illness. The test for society and for the law is whether, in this specific sort of case, the act engaged in has consequences adverse to the peace and welfare of society in general. But when the consequences of the particular conduct are significant only to those immediately involved, society is not interested enough to take notice of it, much less to legally or morally censure it.

The consequences of any action or event can never be fully anticipated or calculated, but that does not prevent society from discriminating between those situations which bluntly and fiercely threaten the common welfare and safety of society, and those which, as far as can be predicted or analyzed, do not. Thus, sexual conduct involving coercion or duress—like rape—is appropriately declared a crime because it so radically endangers human life and is so frequently associated with other extreme, antisocial, often pathological, behavior such as murder or theft. On the other hand, if two unmarried adults in good health, with sensible precautions, in the privacy of a home, and by mutual consent, spend a night together, the foreseeable consequences of such an encounter are so personal and private, pertain so exclusively to the two involved, that society's interest in their conduct should not be asserted to invade their privacy or to censor or curtail their conduct or, least of all, to judge or punish it.

In other words, in any of the realms of sex, society must consider not only the external acts committed or performed, but also the persons involved in those acts—their ages and sexes and maturity and other relationships—and, for that matter, all the other aspects of the specific incident.

SEX AND ADOLESCENCE

Consider, now, the varieties of sexual conduct most characteristic of adolescent life; conduct which is not *intrinsically* antisocial—although in some given instance it may in fact be antisocial or may conceal a latent antisocial problem.

. . . . *petting*

Probably the most typical sexual conduct of adolescents is that discovery, exploration, and enjoyment of sexuality which is evident in necking, petting, and fondling. Such conduct is not in itself antisocial. But where these preliminary, customary, and inherited rituals of sex (so widely displayed in public media—in movies and television, in advertising and magazines—and so much exhibited in the examples of adults) arouse desire or necessity for sexual climax, they are fraught with great perils. These perils include illegitimate births, habituation to a peculiar sexual exercise, grave frustrations or the oppression of guilt, disloyalties to others or the abuse of one's sexual partner. Perils such as these counsel caution in, though they do not forbid, the practices of petting and the like so common in adolescent life.

As a practical matter, however, these perils do not appear to be effective deterrents to adolescent sexual promiscuity. Venereal disease, illegitimate births, and forced marriages because of pregnancies continue to increase greatly both in the city and in the schools and communities outside the city. The methods of solicitation for intercourse by a boy of a girl or by a girl of a boy are common knowledge, at least to adolescents if not to their parents, teachers, or pastors. If a boy, for example, invites a girl to a drive-in movie, she is often accepting an invitation for fondling and, more often

[46]

than not, for intercourse. And both boy and girl homosexual youths have their own signals and insignia.

Where such are the mores of adolescent society, it is hard for a boy or girl to resist conforming to that which everyone else says and does, whether they really want to or not. Conformity here, just as in many other segments of American life, is thought to be synonymous with popularity or at least the price of popularity. Yet conformity is a violence to one's person and personality.

Who are you if you are just like everybody else? I will tell you plainly who you are—*you are nobody!* If you are a conformist just for the sake of being that, it is as if you did not exist in any significant, personal, or human way whatever. It is no real popularity that you gain if your own personality is suffocated in the effort to conform. *You* cannot be popular, much less accepted and loved—which involves a different thing than simple popularity—if you are anonymous, and yet it is anonymity into which conformity invites you. If you are a conformist, if you look and act and talk like everybody else, you are nobody; and if you are nobody you might as well be dead, since you are already dead in principle.

. . . . *cosmetics and clothing*

Nowhere, I suppose, is the tyranny of conformity more obvious in American society than in the use of cosmetics and in the fashions of clothing.

Cosmetics are by no means a modern invention or custom. From primitive times both men and women have used various paints, pigments, and perfumes to adorn their bodies. Cosmetics are one of the inherited rituals of human life, associated not only with sex *per se,* but with class and caste, office, status, wealth, and station. Where the uses of cosmetics are not corrupted (as they are in America) they serve to indicate some sort of position in society or to enhance the beauty of the human body. Of course opinions vary in different societies as to what enhances the beauty of the body. In some societies what would be thought attractive might in another be thought ugly or mutilating. But in our society cosmetics are increasingly used by both women and men to serve the ideal of mass conformity; to make everybody look like everybody else. Usually the standards of conformity in such matters are identified with some public idol such as a movie star or other public figure, and therefore they tend to create a deception. You may be dating a person who is engaged in imitating somebody else, whether that is the intention or the result. There is a great obstacle to actually meeting, much less loving, the real person hidden under the mask. It would be nice to date Cher, but it is not very interesting to date Sally Jones when she is disguised as Cher for, in that case, I will end up being with neither Cher nor Sally Jones, but only with some mannequin.

The same problems are related to clothing fashions, but added to them, ironically, is the increasing tendency among the adolescents for clothes to obscure the sexual identity of the person. At least in the city, it becomes more and more difficult to distinguish girls from boys or boys from girls according to how they dress. The fashions of each sex are remarkably similar, each imitative of the other, and this raises the issue of how much Americans are becoming at one and the same time a most sexually conscious people, but also a sexless people who have lost a sense of both what it means to be masculine and what it means to be feminine.

I do not propose to speculate about why this might be the

case in America, or whether it is an especially American problem. I simply observe that, in an atmosphere in which Americans are increasingly indoctrinated into the same ideas, attitudes, and practices of all sorts, conformity is also at work in making boys and girls and men and women more and more indistinguishable at least in their outward appearance.

. . . . *pornography*

Conformity is probably an indication of both the suppression of sexuality and the profound insecurity among young people and others as to their sexual identity. But a word should be added about another form of sexual suppression which has wide currency among adolescents in America—pornography.

Pornographic pictures and literature should not be confused with erotica. As the courts in both England and America have repeatedly held, erotica is the artistically significant portrayal, pictorially or verbally, of the reality, integrity, and beauty of sexual relationships. Pornography, in contrast, portrays abnormal or atypical sexual activity in a fashion that is provocative, dehumanizing, and obscene. Pornography and pseudo-pornography are easily accessible and widely circulated among young people nowadays and have the proportions of a major commercial enterprise. There are questions for society and the law to consider about how this traffic can be controlled in order that it not mislead or corrupt young people, without at the same time destroying the civil rights of both those who market and those who purchase pornography.

But the more important question may have to do with why pornographic materials have such a ready market among youth. Part of the matter surely is the very secrecy, the clandestine nature, of receiving such materials. And part of it is, I suppose, just curiosity about sex which is whetted by discussions of sex and by the sublimation of sexual conduct at the behest of parents or Church. If sex in all of its meanings, practices, and rituals is not in the open— frankly recognized, intelligently considered, and compassionately dealt with—then what is to be expected except that sex will be the subject of gossip, rumor, escapism, fantasy, and the lure of that which is forbidden? Recourse to pornography among adolescents is, as far as I can discern, far less the consequence of racketeer activities or abnormal adolescent preoccupation with sex than of the fear of candor about sex among adults, including parents and pastors.

. . . . *masturbation*

Another common, in fact, virtually universal variety of sexual experience characteristic of adolescent life is masturbation. Here, too, there is nothing inherently antisocial in the act. But one who persists into adulthood in the practice of masturbation is likely to be one who remains profoundly immature sexually, fearing actual sexual contact with a partner, becoming and being sexually retarded. The main danger and damage in masturbation is not in the conduct itself, but in the fantasy life that invariably accompanies the conduct. That life will hardly ever be a sexually fulfilling one, and indeed masturbation is probably most obviously another variety of sexual sublimation—one in which the sexual identity and capability of the person remains stalemated, indefinite, confused, and apparently self-contained. Masturbation is not antisocial *per se,* but the deep suppression of sexuality which it represents will frequently provoke some other superficially nonsexual, antisocial behavior. And even if the sublimation of masturbation is never relieved, either in sexual relationship with another human being or in some antisocial, apparently non-sexual behavior, the real tragedy—the destructive and dehumanizing fact about masturbation—is its obvious unfulfillment and crude futility among the varieties of sexual activity.

. . . . *homosexuality*

Perhaps no sexual issue in American society among adolescents (although also among adults, both male and female) is more the subject of superstition, rejection, gossip, and uncouth humor than homosexuality. Although petting and masturbation seldom come to the attention of the legal authorities (though much to the attention of parents and teachers), homosexuality is often a concern of the law. As in some other cases—notably, in my own experience as a lawyer in narcotics addiction cases—the law regarding homosexuality is very much behind the insights of the medical sciences as to the understanding or treatment of it either personally or socially. In the law the term is loosely used to designate a fantastically diverse range of sexual conduct and identity. Everything from transvestitism, which is a complex and perplexing ailment, to the most casual sexual contact between two youths of the same sex (a contact provoked by curiosity or immaturity, not by compulsion, illness, or physiological disorder) is indiscriminately lumped together and very often dealt with by the law as if they were all the same phenomenon.

Some of the confusion in the law, if not in the public mind, about what homosexuality is has begun to be dispelled by the readiness of the courts in many jurisdictions to heed medical authority and to treat rather than imprison those charged with criminal offenses involving homosexuality.

In spite of this, many people, perhaps essentially church-people, will still find homosexual relations personally incomprehensible, aesthetically abhorrent, and morally reprehensible. Be that as it may, more fundamental issues than those of personal distaste are involved in the practice of homosexuality. Homosexuals are often tempted to suicide, experience desperate identity crises, fall victim to extortion or blackmail, live in fear of exposure and social disgrace, suffer from profound and unabsolved guilt, are readily vulnerable to venereal disease, feel more persecuted than other social minorities, endure the collapse of relationships with parents and families, and—despite lots of sex—perhaps never know love. These are the significant personal and social issues of homosexuality.

SEX AND SIN

None of the acts of sex which society regards as criminal or antisocial, should necessarily be regarded as sin. On the other hand, those forms of conduct that do not fall under the legal or moral censure of society should not be considered free of sin. Society is not the judge of anyone's sin.

Remember, too, that the biblical comprehension of sin is not the proscription of certain kinds of conduct but the usurpation of God's prerogative to judge all human decisions and actions. Every specific act, every thought, word, and deed of every person, institution, and nation is subject to *that* judgment; and *that* judgment is in no way mitigated, altered, or influenced by the opinions of people or the policy of society. To put it a bit differently, the Christian knows and confesses that in all things—in every act and decision—humans are sinners and in no way, by any ingenuity, piety, sanction, or social conformity, may a person escape from the full burden of the power of sin over his or her whole existence.

If one remembers that the self-interest of society in its condemnation of certain conduct is to be distinguished from sin, that God himself is the only judge, and that no person is innocent of sin, then some insight is possible into the reality of sin in sex. That which is sinful in sexual behavior is the failure, refusal, or incapacity to acknowledge and treat one's own self or another as a person. Essentially, sin is the state of existence in which the separation of a person from God means one's own loss of identity and the forfeit of one's relationship with other persons and, in fact, with the whole of creation. Sin is consignment to death, to be cut off from the one in whom all life originates and in whom all life is fulfilled; to be, in fact, cut off from life itself. The power of sin permeates the rituals of sex, in all their varieties—in marriage and out of marriage, among young or old, among male and female—just as it does in all other affairs in this world. Thus it becomes a tribute to death, a sign of the imminence of death in this life.

The vitality of sin in sex is seen in situations where manipulation, punishment, humiliation, or violation of one by another or of one by one's own self is made obvious because of physical or psychological coercion, willful enticement, false promises, fraud, the exchange of money, lust, or possessiveness. However, the dishonoring of the body and person of one's self or another may take subtle forms and may be as much present in sexual conduct approved or condoned by society as in that which is disapproved or condemned.

Yet the Christian more than recognizes the reality of sin

in sex of all sorts. The Christian knows that sex, which is so full of death, may also become a sacrament of the redemption of human life from the power of sin which death is.

SEX AND THE SEARCH FOR SELF

Such is the mystery of sex and love that what in sex may be dehumanizing, depraved, or merely habitual, may become human, sacramental, and sanctified. For sex to be so great an event as that, it is essential for one to know who he is as a person, to be secure in his own identity, and indeed, to love himself.

Too often sex does not have the dignity of a sacramental event because it is thought to be the means of the search for self rather than the expression and communication of one who has already found oneself and is free from resort to sex in the frantic pursuit of identity. It is wrong to assume that sex is in itself some way of establishing or proving one's identity or any resolution of the search for selfhood. One who does not know oneself and seeks to find oneself in sexual experience with another will neither find self nor will he respect the person of a sexual partner. Often enough, the very futility of the search for identity in sex will increase the abuse of both one's own self and one's partner. The pursuit of identity in sex ends in destruction, in one form or another, for both the one who seeks oneself and the one who is used as the means of the search. No one may show another who he or she is; no one may give another life; no one can save another.

How then shall one discover who one is as a human being if sex provides neither the means nor the answer? And how shall one be emancipated from the power of sin in sex and in other realms as well?

In Christ.

In Christ. That means in beholding Christ who is in his own person the true human, the person living in the state of reconciliation with God, within himself, with all men, with the whole of creation.

In Christ. That means in discerning that God ends the search for self by himself coming in this world in search of men. For the person, who knows that he has been found by God no longer has to find self.

In Christ. That means in surrendering to the presence and power of death in all things including sex and, in that event, in the very midst of death, receiving a new life free from the claim of death.

In Christ. That means in accepting the fact of God's immediate and concretely manifest love for human life, including one's own little life. Finding, then, that one's own life is encompassed in God's love for the world.

In Christ. That means in knowing that in the new life which God gives to humans there is no more a separation between who a person is and what a person does. That which one does, in sex or anything else, is the sign of who one is. All that one does become sacraments of new life.

In Christ. That means in realizing radical fulfillment as a person in the life of God in this world; such radical fulfillment that abstinence in sex is a serious option for a Christian though it is never a moral necessity.

In Christ. That means in enjoying God's love for all humanity and all things in each and every event or decision of one's own life.

In Christ. That means in confessing that all life belongs to God, and but for him there is no life at all.

IV.

Work, Witness, and Worship

> If the work which any man has built on the foundation survives, he will receive a reward. If any man's work is burned up, he will suffer loss, though he himself will be saved, but only as through fire.
>
> *I Corinthians 3:14–15*

Work is the common means by which human beings seek to justify their existence.

The legend, in America anyway, is that in either the product or the reward of work a person can find his or her life morally vindicated. Work is considered a virtue if it satisfies the conformities of the ethics of success; if it enriches either in money, possessions, or fame and reputation; or, as a sort of last resort, if it is memorable—if it is honored by one's posterity, even though one may be dead and rotting in the grave.

The most false and frivolous part of the legend is, of course, the notion that anyone given good health, the competitive spirit, a tolerance of compromise, consummate ambition, and a little bit of luck can do anything one sets out to do, or become anyone one wants to become. And, more often than not, a little religion seems to be useful since God is thought to be eager to help those who help themselves.

In America the ethics of success in work place the highest moral significance upon taking care of yourself and your wealth first and, if possible, never taking care of anyone or anything else. The ethics of success here are an ethics of primitive survival in which the profound moral principle is personal self-interest. Mind you, the expression of that self-interest may not appear in the form of ordinary greed for money and property. It may just as likely take other forms: the lust for power *per se* or for the trappings and condiments of power; the pursuit of fame or notoriety; the quest for a modest security, socially and economically, in which equality is attained because, in your stratum of society, everybody both has and does the same things. Whatever the case, the ethics invoked are the same—seek first your own material and empirical welfare and you will think your existence is justified. Perhaps you will also think that you are accepted and admired, envied and feared, and when you are gone, you will be revered.

Since there is no escape from death, and since there is also no salvation from the awful presence of death, then why not at least build a monument of your reputation, notoriety, wealth, or possessions by conforming to these ethics of success? You can at least enjoy what you have while you live and take satisfaction from the prospect that others, whether few or many, will gaze upon your monument when you die and in the years after your death. Make work your monument, the reason for your life, and you will survive your death in some way, until the monument itself crumbles.

Work is the common means by which people seek to justify their existence while they are alive and to sustain their existence, in a fashion, after they die.

In the ordinary experience of men, work is intimately associated with the reality of death. But Christians know that work is related to death in a much more profound way. Christians discern that work is in itself a service to death, and that all the myths about success and security, money and social conformity, monuments and posterity do not explain or resolve the activity of death in work. Christians approach the question of the meaning of work and the relationship of work to the presence and power of death in relation to the work of God in the world. Christians do not see work in terms of some foolish idea of immortality, but rather as a medium in which the power of God over death may be exposed and praised, in which God may be glorified for his triumph over the reign of death. They see the ordinary work people do in the world as a means of witness and, indeed, of worship.

THE MEANING OF WORK

Work is a foretaste—a preliminary experience—of death. That is both the testimony of the Bible and the empirical knowledge of people at work. One need not look far to observe that, for the great multitudes of people throughout the world, work is a harsh, relentless burden. Most people in most of the world live in appalling poverty. Through work they don't better themselves; they merely maintain their own poverty and indebtedness. This is the case not only for the masses of people in India or Haiti, but also in American society among, for example, migrant workers or urban slumdwellers. Indeed, at the present time, one fourth of all Americans live in poverty.

Yet even among those who are not economically poor, work is a great burden. Those whose work consists of serving the great corporate principalities, for instance, are subject to dehumanizing, enslaving, frequently idolatrous claims over their lives. Does anyone seriously suppose that the high-ranking executives involved in the price-fixing scandals in some of America's great corporations are anything but prisoners, no freer than serfs, confined and conformed to the interests of the principalities they serve?

The language of the Bible regarding principalities—the ruling authorities, the angelic powers, the demons, and the like—sounds strange in modern society, but these words in fact refer to familiar realities of contemporary life. The principalities refer to those entities in creation which nowadays are called institutions, ideologies, and images. Thus a nation is a principality. Or the Communist ideology is a principality. Or the public image of a human being, say a movie star or a politician, is a principality. The image or legend of Marilyn Monroe or John F. Kennedy is a reality, distinguishable from the person bearing the same name, which survives and has its own existence apart from the existence of the person.

This too is the biblical description of work. In sin people lose their dominion over the creation which God gave them, and their relationship with this creation becomes toil. ". . . cursed is the ground because of you; in toil you shall eat of it all the days of your life; thorns and thistles it shall bring forth to you; and you shall eat the plants of the field. In the sweat of your face you shall eat bread till you return to the ground, for out of it you were taken; you are dust, and to dust you shall return.'' (Gen. 3:17–19)

Work represents the broken relationship between humans and the rest of creation. People, literally, work to death.

The fallenness of work, the broken relationship between human life and the rest of creation which work is, involves both the alienation from nature and from the rest of creation, including the principalities and powers. In work humans lose their dominion over and are in bondage to the principalities. Instead of human beings ruling the great institutions—corporations, unions, and the like—they are ruled by them. The claim over a person's life that all principalities make is idolatrous; that is, the claim that the significance and destiny of a person depends upon service for the survival and preservation of the principality. The estrangement between human beings and the rest of creation means, among other things, the enslavement of persons to the institutions for which they work.

Choice of work is largely illusory, too. You cannot choose a job that will save you the burden of death in work. The multitudes of the poor in the world do not choose what work they will do if, indeed, there is any work for them to do. But even among more economically secure, somewhat educated people the choice of work is largely determined by factors beyond a person's control, beyond the scope of a person's freedom. Choice is made or coerced by the ethics of conformity—the preferences, prejudices, and traditions of family, class, or race; the idols of status and success; the lust for money and possessions. And where there is some apparent freedom of choice of a job, the essential meaning of work is not changed by the choice.

. . . . *non-work*

Non-work, like work, represents the broken relationship between humanity and the rest of creation and, in American society, non-work is of increasing significance. Non-work in the sense of unemployment continues to plague American life and embodies not only the threat to life in the obvious terms of economic insecurity and instability, but also, and perhaps more importantly, prolonged, enforced idleness which is profoundly debilitating psychologically. Unemployment caused by mandatory retirement of older persons is particularly depressing since it so often marks the beginning of a period in which an unoccupied person is simply waiting for his own death.

Unemployment and unemployability are related to the accelerating impact of automation on urban life. There are, for example, about a quarter of a million elevator operators in this country with no other occupational skill, who are now facing imminent displacement because of the automation of elevators.

Unemployability of vast numbers of people becomes the prospect in many other areas, especially where there are many people working at menial jobs. This is an especially serious problem for young people who have only marginal skills. The ranks of the unemployable of all ages have joined those of the retired, the disabled, and the elderly in non-work, in awaiting death.

. . . . *leisure*

The most elementary and common form of non-work is, of course, leisure—the time and activities in which people occupy themselves when not at work. The broken relationship between human life and the rest of creation is evident here also. The breach that work creates is not healed during leisure time, especially not in a society such as ours where leisure is mainly consumed by highly organized activities designed to fill time. The hypnotic addiction to gazing at a television set at every opportunity, day after day and night after night, is but the crudest example. There are also those leisure activities pursued in response to commercial indoctrination which instructs a person of a certain status as to what he must have or do to maintain his place in society: if you are of one class you must play golf, if from another you must bowl, if from another you must drink scotch, if from another you must join a dance studio, and so on. Leisure has become the commercial exploitation of boredom. It is as much an anticipation of death, as much an enslavement to the world, as work is.

. . . . products and rewards

As for the products and rewards of work, they suffer the same end as the worker. They perish, and nothing in or about them has any saving power against the reality of death. It is vain to suppose that either work or non-work, both representing the alienation of humans from the rest of creation, has any efficacy against the power of death's reign. Neither work nor non-work justifies the worker.

There is no sense in which one can find moral justification in work, despite much talk in the churches to that effect. The burden of work, which is the threat of death, is neither mitigated nor overcome in the choice, product, or rewards of work, in non-work, in the moral vanity of work.

THE WORK OF GOD FOR THE WORLD

For Christians, work—the analysis of its meaning, the concrete problems of work, the personal experience of work—

must be understood in the context of the work of God in the world.

For non-Christians, it may seem an impertinence for Christians to speak of God's work at all.

It is.

It is the very boldness of confession of the gospel; it is the confession that God has spoken for himself and that he addresses humans in a way that enables them to witness to what he has said and done.

Or it may seem superfluous to non-Christians to speak of the work of God in connection with the work of humans. It is enough to deal with one or the other without mixing the two. But this is the very foolishness which announces that the only true work of human beings is witness to the work of God.

What really scandalizes non-Christians is the confession on the part of Christians that God lives and *works*: that is the awful scandal of the gospel. To confess God in this way is not an affection for "moral and spiritual values" nor is it a persuasion to some splendid idea of God; it is not just a religious vocabulary dressing up ordinary social morality, nor is it some sublime speculative truth; but it is confession of God's real presence—his life, power, vitality, action, and work in and for this world.

Thus the critical question about work concerns the identity of Jesus Christ and the work of God in him for the world. Who is Jesus Christ? What is the work of God in him for the world? The work of God in Christ for the world *is the world*. The work of God in Christ is God making the world for himself. The original and final, the indigenous and present, the fundamental and radical truth about creation is the lordship of Jesus Christ. Christ is Lord: the world and the work of the world in which men and women engage belong to him. Christ is Lord: in him is the embodiment of human life which is reconciled within itself and at the same time with both God and all things and all persons.

The work of God in Christ for the world is *God vindicating himself in the world*. The hostility of the world to God, the futility of the work of the world in and of itself, the perishing of humans in their work, the demands of the principalities—none of these threaten or depose Christ as Lord. On the contrary, they confirm his lordship, for in him God has triumphed over them. In our history, in Christ, God accepts and assumes the fullness of the burden of the rejection of both persons and nations. Specifically and climactically in the Crucifixion, he manifests decisively his own identity and power in God and, at the same time, affirms and renews the lives of the people in this world.

The work of God in Christ for the world is *God restoring fallen creation to himself*. In Christ God takes upon himself the whole burden of the hostility of the world to him, the futility of work, and even the immediate and ultimate powers of death itself. Thereby are people set free, in both their lives and work, from the threat of death and from the homage death seeks. In Christ there is a new creation. In Christ there is a new birth for human beings. In Christ God elects the Church, constitutes for himself a new people who are saved from death. In Christ the world is absolved from the Fall—from the reign of death—and the integrity of creation is rescued and restored.

The work of God in Christ for the world is *God judging the world*. In Christ the mercy of God in reconciling the world to himself is the event by which the world is judged. Where the Church represents the world reconciled to God, where the Church lives as Christ's Body, where the Church heralds the judgment of the world by Christ, the Church suffers the same hostility of the world that Christ himself bore. In that sense the Church, in the midst of her service to and mission in the world, always stands over against the world representing in her own historic life the society that the world is called to be. The Church is thus the exemplification of the work of God for the world.

The work of God in Christ for the world is *God ending the world*. In Christ is God bringing all things and all men to their fulfillment and to their end in himself. Christ is Lord: as Christ is the beginning, so Christ is the end. The Church lives in constant expectancy of and in readiness for the consummation of the world in Christ, not for the sake of herself, but for the sake of the world.

WORK AS WITNESS

The work of God in Christ for the world is accomplished in *this* world, in the very world in which men live and work and are dying, in this world which people know from their own ordinary experience. That means that those who witness to God's work in this world are given freedom to confront and cope with the world as it is, without romanticism; without indifference to any actual experience of people at work; without rationalization; without imagining that the world is different from what it is; without evasion; without escape from the real burden of daily work, which is the very burden of death. A mark of the Christian witness is an invariable, unfeigned realism about the world and the work of the world.

For one to be free in work or in non-work—free from merely working to death, free from enslavement to the principalities and powers—one must be set free from the bondage to death. It is the work of God in Christ for the world that frees people from this bondage and that enables any secular work to become and to be a witness to the work of God.

In other words, for Christians who take seriously the work of Christ for the world, the question of work is not an essentially ethical one. It is a *confessional* one. The problem is not the moral significance of the daily work of people to God but, rather, the meaning of the work of God for the common work of human beings. For the Christian, work is not what people do for God's sake or their own, but a witness to what God does for the sake of all and for the sake of the whole world.

However, one must not forget that even Christians, perhaps as often as non-Christians, minimize or ignore the work of God when they discuss the work of people in the world. The evidence for this is common enough in church literature on vocation and work, where there is so much talk of "applying faith to daily work" or of "making the gospel relevant to secular work." Coming from Christians this is astonishing, for in the Christian faith there is no inherent problem in connecting a god who is someplace else—a god of abstract presence and power—with this world. Nor is there any issue of relating a gospel which is about something else—a hypothetical or idealistic gospel—to the life and work of this world. Christ means God in the world. The gospel of Christ means the work of God in the world for the world. Christ means the creative, comprehensive, specific, and conclusive concern of God for the common life and work of this world.

When Christians do overlook the work of God, they risk a disintegration of the Christian life in the world and an immobilization of the Christian mission for the world. Where there is such oversight the understanding of Christian vocation in daily work becomes, at most, a mere attempt to formulate and articulate some ethics of decision for daily work.

Work as witness is specifically the confession of the

lordship of Christ through ordinary daily work. That is, the whole of creation, despite its fallenness, belongs to God. The fact of Christ's lordship over the whole of life, including work, means that witness is the only proper work of humans and any employment or occupation may be the instrument of that work.

In Christ is the image of human dominion over the rest of creation which God first gives in creation and which is lost in sin. And for those who become members of the Body of Christ in the world, dominion is restored. The Christian is a person who, by the work of Christ, has had his or her own life restored, is free from the threat of death in all things, and now lives in reconciliation with other people and with the rest of creation.

WORK AS WORSHIP

For such a human being, daily work and non-work become virtually indistinguishable from worship. Worship is not some peculiar cultic practice, some esoteric folk activity to which Christians resort out of sentiment or superstition for inspiration or self-motivation. On the contrary, worship is the celebration of God's presence and action in the ordinary and everyday life of the world. Worship is not separate or distinguishable from the rest of the Christian life; it is the normative form and expression of the Christian life; it is the integration of the whole of the Christian life into history.

The actions and relationships characteristic of the gathered, sacramental life of the Church in worship are the precedent for the actions and relationships of members of the company of the Church in their involvement in the common life of the world. At the same time, the specific involvement of Christians in the life and work of the world every day is that which they offer to God in the corporate worship of the Church. One validates the other. Neither can exist, with integrity and meaning, without the other. Worship in the sanctuary is empty unless the Christian in his daily work is engaged in acknowledging and celebrating the work of God for the world. But daily work is not sanctified unless it is offered, encompassed, taken up into the worship of the whole people of the Church in their gathering in the sanctuary.

In the Christian faith, unlike the practices of some other religions, worship does not mean offering to God what it is thought would please or appease him. In the gospel, human beings do not sacrifice themselves for God. On the contrary, in the gospel God sacrifices his life for human beings. (That is why there is really no such thing as martyrdom in the Christian faith.) What Christians offer God in worship, both in the sanctuary and in daily work, is everything—the whole of their lives, all that they have said and done, that which seems good and worthy of themselves as well as that which seems to them evil or unworthy. It is for God's mercy alone to determine what is pleasing to him. Christians only know that God cares for the uttermost of a person's life, and claims the whole of a person's life, with nothing reserved, nothing held back, nothing to hide, no matter what.

When worship is the style and meaning of all that a person is and does, when everything in work, play, talk, deed, or thought is included in the offertory—then is one free from the intimidations of death. Then a person knows and confesses that it is God in whom all life is given, received, and made whole.

V.

Justification, the Consumption Ethic, and Vocational Poverty

For you know the grace of our Lord Jesus Christ, that though he was rich, yet for your sake he became poor, so that by his poverty you might become rich. And in this matter I give my advice: it is best for you now to complete what a year ago you began not only to do but to desire, so that your readiness in desiring it may be matched by your completing it out of what you have. . . . I do not mean that others should be eased and you burdened, but that as a matter of equality your abundance at the present time should supply their want, so that their abundance may supply your want, that there may be equality.

II Corinthians 8:9–11, 13–14

Though the inherited American work ethic has neither biblical origin nor rationale, there was a certain coherence in attributing significance to human labor in pre-industrial society. Where the toil of human beings was tangibly productive (the result being a harvested crop, the construction of a shelter, the furnishing of a household, or the making of clothing) it was understandably appealing to consider work to be proof of a person's virtue and moral worth.

Before industrialization, work was so closely associated with the effort to survive that one can understand why work was regarded as the common means of justification. In circumstances in which work so literally involved sweat, burden, coercion, exhaustion, and pain, attaching a theological connotation promised relief from premonitions of death. Moreover, the notion that the tangible products of work were evidence of moral worth was reinforced by the idea that the privileged classes—those of inherited property and station—ruled by divine right. Their propertied status and their privileges verified their moral superiority.

This pagan, unbiblical work ethic—though it found expression in established Catholicism, Lutheranism, and Calvinism when each of these became vested in the *status quo;* in Anglicanism during the period of British exploration and colonization; and in Puritan pietism and its derivatives—greatly abetted the oppression and brutalization of human beings. In feudal societies, for example, this doctrine of work was invoked to deprive the peasantry of the products of their labor by offering them the fearsome inducement that their bondage was ordained by God. Similarly, during the time of chattel slavery in America, an embellishment of the same doctrine promised a dutiful slave freedom from work in an indefinite heavenly realm to which access could be gained only through his endurance of servility in this world. The servitude of women and children, the policy of Indian genocide in the colonial settlements and later on the frontier, the successive exploitations of immigrants are all related to variations of this work ethic.

THE IMPACT OF INDUSTRIALIZATION

Industrialization, even in its most primitive stages, wrought extraordinary changes which rendered the traditional work doctrine incoherent. The most visible aspect of these changes was that affecting the products of work. This represents change which is still taking place, with the enormous added impetus of technology, in post-industrial societies like the United States. Part of the change occasioned by the industrial revolution was the new capability of producing a surplus of tangible goods. Industrialization meant a potential for producing more than was immediately needed for mere survival. Consequently, there were new possibilities for managing supplies, manipulating costs, fixing prices, and hoarding for gluttony and waste.

A key to the changes inherent in the industrial process was distribution. The capacity to produce enough for all— for those who worked, as well as those who ruled or were otherwise privileged—meant that workers could share, beyond the terms of bare existence, in the products of their own labor. The justifying virtue of their work was no longer subject to unrequited patience or indeterminate postponement. Thus, if distribution were affected, consumption could also be radically altered. The consuming class might no longer be restricted to people of inherited privileges and the bankers, merchants, and traders beholden to them, but could also include the producing class, the workers, the lumpen proletariat. In America, it was predicted that the proletariat would become part of the bourgeoisie because mechanization would displace menial labor and the distribution of products would be perfected.

What has spoiled this myth is the capability, through industrialization, of producing a superfluity of products. As industrialization became more and more sophisticated and was overtaken by technology, the main trend became the priority of luxury over necessity in production, distribution, and consumption.

Although, since the advent of industrialization in America, the harshness of work has been somewhat eased for the laborer, compared to the lot to which their predecessors were consigned, the change has also been accompanied by other, more negative developments of great significance to the traditional work ethic. One of these is the proliferation of intangible work—activity included within the realm socially and economically defined as work, but which does not produce tangible goods of any sort. So there have multiplied (geometrically) lenders, brokers, agents, managers, middlemen, transporters, packagers, salespeople, merchandisers, handlers, promoters, bureaucrats, facilitators, consultants, insurers, advertisers; in short, a profuse and complex array of personnel engaged in forms of work unimagined before industrialization. With that, a shift has occurred in the concept of work from the earlier focus upon products to that upon rewards. Work has been redefined; it is no longer simply associated with productive labor but is defined as activity, *any* activity for which compensation is paid, whether or not it is tangibly productive.

Soon work defined as compensated activity became work designated by consumption; products which could be acquired and controlled through payment of some sort. The transposition has been from productivity to compensation and from compensation to consumption. With that extraordinary change in the meaning of work, the familiar work ethic has also been recast so that justifying significance, earlier imputed to productive work, is now attached to compensation and consumption. What has been lost in the process is moral discrimination between utility and uselessness, between necessity and luxury, between human need and profligate consumption.

A good example of the application of this notion of justification associated with the consumption ethic can be recalled in the first public remarks made by a President of the United States about the so-called energy crisis. It was prominent in one of those homilies which Richard Nixon used to utter with such mock earnestness, during the winter oil embargo of 1973-4. Nixon then urged that the nation seek "self-sufficiency" in energy supplies. America, he observed, consumed more than a third of the world's energy resources, much of it for what elsewhere would be regarded as luxury, but which in America had become necessity, since its lifestyle demonstrated the moral superiority of American society. Mr. Nixon's abdication has yielded no fundamental challenge to this teaching, either as economics or as theology.

RHETORIC AND MYTH

This points to the importance of the rhetorical and mythological aspects of the quest for justification of the consumption ethic in American society. There is an intimacy between rhetoric and myth, a tension of incantation between the two; the one invokes the other in indefinite reciprocity until the relationship of either to empirical reality vanishes. As I mentioned earlier, the work ethic of the pre-industrial era had a certain plausibility, albeit biblically unsupported; but that is dissipated when the old work ethic is applied to "work" in an advanced technocratic state. If this is not generally perceived by contemporary Americans, it is rhetoric and the mythology it sponsors, and myth and the rhetoric it fosters, which hinders their insight.

Thus, although the nature and definition of work have changed, the rhetoric of the inherited work doctrine has been preserved and its mythology has become elaborately embellished. The most persuasive part of the proposition that work proves moral worth was the tangible productivity of work, especially where the products of work were necessary for human survival: providing shelter, clothing, health, food, or safety. In the American technocracy, that very rationale is disappearing as work becomes merely unproductive, compensated activity and, at the same time, increasingly useless or harmful as far as the sustenance of human life is concerned.

The adaptation of the early work ethic to the conditions of primitive industrialization was initially accomplished in two ways: first, by extending the myth concerning the "sanctity" of private property and the consequent priority of property over human life; and, secondly, by the invention of the creedal lexicon of *laissez faire* capitalism with its familiar articles about "individual initiative," "free enterprise," "the profit motive," and "the law of supply and demand." It was to such symbols as these that the way of justification was to be attributed, a fact curiously attested to in the common reference nowadays to these very ideas as "the old time religion."

However, private property—in the classic meaning of the ownership of land or slaves—has long since virtually disappeared. Today, and for a long time before today, people have owned mortgages, banks have owned land, chattel slavery has been abolished, and *laissez faire* capitalism has been extinguished since the First World War (some would place the date earlier, questioning whether it ever existed at all, given the traditional manipulation of public funds by private entrepreneurs from the outset of industrialization in America). Yet, as radically diminished as the ownership of private property may be and as extinct as *laissez faire* capitalism is, the archaic shibboleths attending property and capitalism remain alive.

The fabric of rhetoric and mythology—"the old time religion"—has not lost its ability to achieve the oppression of human life. If, in earlier days, imputing justification to human labor appeased, frightened, benighted, or otherwise subjugated serfs and slaves, women and children, it is much the same now. Today it is common belief that compensation determines moral worth and, thus, to be uncompensated or undercompensated betrays moral deficiency. The public doctrine is that not working, which only means not being compensated, is a state of sin. To verify that, reread any presidential remark on welfare recipients given since 1968. Not only does this teaching distort or ignore the truth about racism, deprived education, the institutionalization of unemployability among dispossessed Americans; not only does it falsely, indiscriminately, and categorically denounce the abilities and aspirations of those consigned to the welfare system; not only does it render welfare recipients scapegoats for compounded failures of this society to provide training and opportunity for employment; but it also refuses to recognize how much of the effort and activity of the poor, of those uncompensated or undercompensated, actually subsidizes those who are employed, duly compensated, and deemed affluent. In a society in which compensation defines work, an issue arises about the extent to which work that is socially necessary or useful is not compensated but ought to be (without implying any moral delinquency such as occurs, given the vitality of "the old time religion," under the existing welfare policy). Is not housework work? Is not the care of children work? Is not study or apprenticeship work? Is not contending with bureaucracy work? Is not searching for a job work? For that matter, is not coerced unemployment work? There is much work done in this society which is not socially recognized or economically rewarded as work, according to the prevailing conception of work. The issue extends not only to many welfare recipients, to the poor in general, to blacks, to Indians, to Chicanos, but also to multitudes of older citizens—to those living in enforced retirement, consigned to a second childhood—and some people in their first childhood (adolescents) as well. Where work is supposed to offer moral justification and is confined to the incident of compensation, those who are compensated (the so-called affluent classes) perhaps need dependent classes to whom they can ascribe moral inferiority in order to fortify their fragile claim to moral superiority. Such is the function of rhetoric and myth.

THE CONSUMPTION ETHIC

To state the matter so baldly may not only illustrate the potency of both rehtoric and mythology, but also expose the incongruity of the attempt to apply the pre-industrial work ethic to compensated activity in an advanced technocracy like the United States. The absurdity is all the more obvious when one takes into account that developments by technocrats have increasingly shifted the symbol of justification in work from compensation to consumption. Where the concept of work is narrowed to compensated effort, the moral worthiness of the one compensated is evidenced in that which compensation facilitates. If acquisitiveness once had such a connotation—the amassing of personal fortune, the purchase of conspicuous luxuries, the control of investment holdings, or the like—this has lately diminished as compared to consumption *per se*. Now, compensation mainly enables consumption and consumption displays the virtue or the justified status of the consumer.

The difficulty with the transformation from compensation to consumption is that technology not only has the distinctive capability to make that which will be consumed, but it also has the capability to determine what will be consumed. In principle, technology—specifically the technology of propaganda, promotion, advertising, packaging, and marketing—can program human beings to consume indiscriminately: to consume what they do not need, what they do not rationally want, what they cannot use, what will not enhance human living, and, indeed, even what will jeopardize life. A tour of any supermarket or discount house in any shopping center confirms this, but the pervasiveness of the manipulation of human beings as consumers has corrupted everything in the marketplace.

In publishing, which has had a reputation for the spread of literacy and the patronage of creativity, studies show that book sales can be induced according to the color and design features of the book jacket, regardless of the topic or contents of the volume. In other words, as with so many items on supermarket shelves, it is the *package* which is sold. The implication is ominous, for on the day on which the big commercial enterprises—many of them now controlled by conglomerates—learned that consumers could be conditioned to purchase the book jacket instead of the book, the prospects for creative writing and literacy were drastically minimized.

The automobile is the archetypical example of profligate consumption, as distinguished from simple acquisitiveness caused by the impact of technocracy upon consumption. Once upon a time, the automobile could be regarded as a means of transportation which enabled the mobility of human beings and facilitated the distribution of goods. It offered an enhanced freedom for human life—in educational and employment opportunities, recreation, and freedom from want. But that promise began to be frustrated and spoiled in America when the making and marketing of automobiles became dominated by proponents of indiscriminate consumption.

Thus, necessity and utility have been overwhelmed by the identification of the automobile as a symbol of class status, sexual energy, autonomous power, aggressive instinct, separation and isolation, and escape. Function becomes secondary to design, safety becomes secondary to appearance; waste (being a "two car family" or a "three car family") is introduced and encouraged, obsolescence is planned. All that followed from that point was more or less predictable: the overproduction of cars so saturated the highway system that the elementary purpose of the vehicle was refuted—transportation was not facilitated but strangulated; the environment was damaged, health was jeopardized, safety was neglected, the public expense of subsidizing the level of overproduction occasioned the neglect of urgent social problems, the police power and presence in society was further escalated, tens of thousands of ancillary enterprises and the employment they furnished proliferated.

The day has come when overproduction and profligate consumption of the automobile, as in the parallel operation of the war ethic, poses a fatal dilemma for this society: we cannot live humanly if the basic premise of indefinitely expanding production and consumption of the car prevails. However, we cannot abandon that premise without suffering the most radical dislocation, especially that affecting employment which has become so dependent on it.

AFFLUENCE AS THE NEW POVERTY

In the aftermath of the reputed energy crisis, this profound quandary has become quite evident. There has been a sharp decline in auto sales and an enormous amount of unemployment in the industry and its multifarious satellites. If people now apprehend an American apocalypse, they will not be much mistaken. We are beginning to perceive that the penultimate implementation of the consumption ethic is self-consumption. This is not an aphorism but, rather, a practical statement. In the case of America it means that, in the progression by which compensation enables consumption for the sake of consumption, a gap will sooner or later appear. For the compensated classes—the so-called affluent —there comes a time when consumption has been conditioned to be so indiscriminate and so insatiable that it can no longer be sustained by the compensation available. That deficiency is filled by credit; by access for the ''affluent'' to easy, if expensive, credit. In the acceleration of this chain, it soon becomes obvious that compensation facilitates credit and credit supports consumption. If, initially, this amended syllogism seems to satisfy the gap between compensation and consumption, it does so through illusion. The operation of the consumption ethic is so enthralling and so relentless that, at last, credit—no more than compensation—is sufficient. Thus, the absurd reality emerges in which the compensated classes of society, in order to maintain the consumption which supposedly verifies their superior moral status, become so overburdened with debt that they are poorer than those classes officially labeled "the poor."

Affluence in America is a new kind of poverty. This is a poverty which renders its victims very vulnerable to conforming pressures of every sort; especially so in politics by acquiescing to a totalitarian rule which offers to protect the consumption of the affluent by escalating the persecution of the official poor. The defamation, harassment, and deprivation of the poor become more prominent as the vanity of the affluent is threatened and the new poverty of the consuming classes is exposed. All that has lately been in evidence during the great recession/inflation of the seventies in which the so-called affluent—having endorsed the fiction that poverty is sin—have begun to suffer the practical realities of their own poverty and the haunting anxiety that their consumption will be curtailed and, thus, their virtue lost.

A VOCATIONAL POVERTY

The distention of the American consumption ethic has occasioned the rebellion of multitudes of citizens, most conspicuously, but by no means exclusively, among the young. An ostentatious sign of such sentiments—one which allows for "affluence" as a form of poverty—is the new uniform of younger Americans, particularly the offspring of the white middle classes: the prematurely patched jeans, second-hand clothes, or workman's overalls. Moreover, there has been a plethora of attempts to find a different style of life or at least to escape from the status consigned to the compensated classes. There are communities, communes, extended families, and *ad hoc* households which seek to establish enclaves of civility or piety outside the chaos which the established order symbolizes. Alternatives in education, transportation, communication, recreation, diet, and occupation are experimented with. If much of this is nostalgic, tending merely to fictionalize the past or to simulate poverty, I, for one, volunteer no critique of this simulated poverty beyond noticing that these efforts are pathetic because they are a private coping or simple protest and have little effect on the society in general. Although they represent options for a few people, they are not open to enough to portend a basic social reconstruction. No greening of America is happening; nor is one likely to take place. Meanwhile, as in the suppression of the black revolt in the sixties which institutionalized urban apartheid, the overwhelming retaliatory capability marshalled in the technocratic state has rendered revolution, in its classical sense, impractical and quaint.

The nominal character of these gestures may not discredit them, but their fraility and poignancy magnify the need to address the American social crisis in proportion to its scope and complexity and, specifically, in corporate and institutional terms, rather than solitary or scattered ways. Organic gardening in the backyard may be a commendable endeavor, but it does not diminish the domination of the principalities of agra-business in the American economy. Only an institution can confront, challenge, rebuke, and (to use a New Testament image) *engage in warfare* with the principalities and powers, institutions and structures, bureaucracies and authorities which constitute the technocratic regime which rules American society. Corrupt and lethargic though it is in its present form, the institution which has that capacity, as a matter of vocation, is the Church of Jesus Christ.

The precedent of this institutional vocation of the Church is pre-Constantinian—coming before the era of Christendom, wherein the Church acquired so solemn an interest vested in the *status quo* of politics and economics. Indeed, the precedent is biblical. No recent change caused by industrialization or technology has essentially altered the hostility, aggression, and anti-human purpose of the powers and principalities of the Church as a society and institution, as disclosed in the *Acts of the Apostles*. Although the nomenclature, appearance, or comprehension of these principalities may have changed in these twenty centuries or so, the fallen character of these powers has not. The principalities militant on the American scene today are no more or less potent and fearful. Nor has the grace and audacity with which the Church, if the Church is to be faithful, is called to confront and rebuke the ruling institutions changed since the genesis of the Church at Pentecost.

The Church is summoned by the word of God now, as then, to a vocation of poverty as an *institution*. And now, as then, that means the radical disassociation of the Church from the prevailing order, from the *status quo*, from the ruling powers, from the established institutions of finance and politics, property and commerce, consumption and war. The disassociation is not occasioned by the circumstance that the American society is perishing, but, rather, is inherent in the vocation of the Church; it is integral to the nature of the Church as the expectant and pioneer society; it is basic to understanding the Church as the herald in this world of the Kingdom of God; it is essential to the Church living, literally, under the sovereignty of the word of God and in anticipation of the judgment of the word of God for this world.

So the vocation of poverty means disassociation from privilege, from power, from property. To be quite specific, it requires the Church's renunciation of such vested interests as tax exemption so that, as an institution, it can be free to practice tax resistance. It also requires the divestiture of endowments and investments from the predatory regime of the corporations, conglomerates, and the entire complex of assorted commercial, military, and scientific principalities which now cripple the Church's humanity. It means the unqualified expendability of every resource that the institutional Church draws upon in its care for the evident, empirical needs of human life in society for health, education, employment, or play. If that renders the familiar fabric of the Church—the churchly sanctuaries and the like—monuments or museums only, then so be it.

Thus, the disassociation from prerogative which marks the vocational poverty of the Church as an institution is no drop-out or withdrawal, no retreat or escape. It represents, rather, the Church's profound engagement in the world as it is. It is the help which the Church freely and gladly offers in the midst of impending disaster.

VI.

Technocracy, Politics and the Resistance Witness

Yet among the mature we do impart wisdom, although it is not a wisdom of this age or of the rulers of this age, who are doomed to pass away. But we impart a secret and hidden wisdom of God, which God decreed before the ages for our glorification. None of the rulers of this age understood this; for if they had, they would not have crucified the Lord of glory.

I Corinthians 2:6–8

T he aftermath of the prolonged war in Southeast Asia and of the coinciding political crisis which has come to be symbolized in the name "Watergate" furnish temptation for most Americans to oversimplify the present situation and wrongly perceive the prospects for their society.

There is an accrued fatigue from these ordeals and scandals which yearns for respite, as well as the pent-up frustrations which find expression in cynicism and quietism. But besides such sentiments, there is the tendency to exaggerate the villainy of Presidents, military and intelligence professionals, and other public officers as if their stupidity or malice, their practical incompetence or moral turpitude, their criminality or vanity were enough to account for the plight of the nation. Thus people hallucinate: they assume that war is over even though the war establishment is as deeply entrenched as ever, even though the war enterprise has become more heavily financed since the formal conclusion in Vietnam, and even though the war policy of America is more reckless now because the war in Indochina meant an American failure of disastrous magnitude. Or they imagine that the constitutional and political crisis was exposed, climaxed, and resolved in the prosecution of a few Watergate personalities and in the resignation of Richard Nixon, even though the unlawful excesses of the Nixon presidency and the criminal offenses of the Nixon cabal are known not to have been unique, and even though, in the case of Nixon himself, the constitutional process was aborted.

I do not deny the necessity of accounting for the public villains; indeed, I regret that such was not accomplished as is proven, with respect to war, by the Calley case and, with respect to Watergate, by the Nixon pardon. Yet I do suggest that both the Indochina war and the Watergate uproar represent symptoms rather than causes, and that, in the disposal of both of these situations, the essential American crisis has not been confronted, much less settled. The grave temptation for Americans today is to feel that "the system has worked" or that it has somehow been incongruously vindicated; hence we overlook the truth of how the system has radically, perhaps irrevocably, changed. Not only do Vietnam and Watergate merely represent symptoms, but the American crisis as a nation and a society is such that, had these not happened at all, Americans would nonetheless find themselves in much the same circumstances.

AN AMERICAN COUNTER-REVOLUTION

Since the Second World War, when technology superseded industrialization as the dominant institutional and ideological power in society, America has been suffering a counterrevolution of extraordinary scope and consequence. One of its most conspicuous features is the proliferation of *extraconstitutional* agencies and authorities which, taking into account their complex social, economic, and political impact, become the effectual regime of the nation, displacing the rule of the inherited governmental institutions and usurping the rule of law as such.

This is a counter-revolution in the classical sense of the term. That is, the effort is the undoing of the political and social ethic of the American Revolution or, at least, of that aspect of the societal ethic of the revolution which em-

[89]

bodied a policy which values human life. The ethical origins of the nation can be seen as ambiguous because they contain so much that renders property, as a social ethic, more basic than the concern for human life. It may be argued that technology and the technocracy that it supports are an implementation, in extremely elaborate and sophisticated terms, of the primitive property ethic which was so prominent in the settling and founding of the nation. Whatever the truth about such a proposition, the reality in this past quarter century or so has been the emergence of such a militant technology that the historic tension between the property ethic and the priority of human life has been practically surpassed. The political development of technology has produced a form of government which virtually abolishes that familiar tension by its destruction of human rights, its coercion of human life, its domination of human beings; in short, by its undoing of that part of the constitutional fabric which values human life in society. Technology has installed a counter-revolutionary regime—a technocratic totalitarianism—which has set aside, if not literally overturned, the inherited constitutional institutions thereby creating a vested ruling authority outside the law and beyond accountability to people.

I do not want to be indefinite about my meaning: I am referring to the remarkable principalities that have proliferated since the Second World War such as the Pentagon, the C.I.A., the F.B.I., and the whole array of secret police and security agencies, as well as the private principalities—the multinational corporations, the conglomerates, and the utilities—which are politically associated with the military, intelligence, and police powers. I am talking about the famous military-industrial-scientific complex which, in its operation as a clandestine second government, is outside the realm of law or accountability to those who are governed or the American Constitution; which has neutralized, obviated, or captivated the publicly designated government.

Hence, I question the accuracy of those who have been saying, in the wake of war and Watergate, that the American political crisis is focused in the "imperial presidency" and that a semblance of democracy might be restored by resurrection of the Congress or reduction of excesses of presidential power. The expansion of presidential power has been largely theatrical and superficial, nourishing the impression that the President governs. In reality, the President's part in policy-making—as is documented by the way in which the budget is determined—has sharply diminished, while the policy initiative of the Pentagon bureaucracy, the so-called intelligence community, and some of the great corporate powers has fantastically increased. If Vietnam proved nothing else, it proved that the nation is not governed by the constitutional system, that public policy is not wrought in the White House, much less the Congress, and that the President and the presidency as an institution are more in the position of victim or captive of an *ad hoc* ruling technocracy than in political control.

AN INHERENT LAWLESSNESS

American technocratic totalitarianism is, from the point of view of a constitutional system, inherently lawless. The morality which dominates the functioning of this array of principalities conjoined in the military-industrial-scientific complex is the survival of the principalities. Everything and everyone else is sacrificed to that overwhelming goal. The principalities of technocracy are predatory. If there is some human benefit that arises out of their political ascendancy, it is either incidental or illusory, a means by which people are further enthralled and demeaned. The stereotypical claim —sponsored in one version by the military establishment, in another by the police power—is that human freedom cannot be politically honored because "security" would be jeopardized. In context, "security" can refer to "the national security"—a concept which may have had some validity during the Second World War but, as used today by the military establishment, has deteriorated into a vague, ritualistic term used to intimidate citizens opposed to adventurism, waste, or aggrandisement of the Pentagon's political and economic power. Or, in relation to the escalation of the internal police power, "security" commonly means the protection of official or corporate property, the convenience of technical procedure or routine, or the conditioning of people to exist in fear ("for their own safety") whether or not any empirical basis for fright is warranted. Amidst the multifarious variations of the excuse for "security," the central consequence is the same: the exercise of human rights is removed because it is an impediment to the operation of lawless authority. The same "security" issue was used to justify both the illegality of the war in Indochina and the unconstitutional surveillance and harassment of the thousands of citizens who sought to expose the genocide there.

It is significant that the burden of the anti-war protests, notably that part informed by the conscience of Christians, was both theologically traditional and politically conservative. The official defamations which portrayed the Christian opposition to the war—exemplified by the Berrigan brothers—as a movement of extreme radicalism or perverse rebellion were categorically false. These Christian protesters understood that the war was both criminal and unconstitutional and that it was being waged through illegitimate political authority which Christian people are called in the New Testament to resist. In political terms, the effort was to expose and oppose a lawless counter-revolutionary regime so that the constitutional system might be restored in America—an authentic conservative cause, indeed.

In the light of that, of course, the Christian anti-war protests would have to be considered failures, since the end of combat for Americans has not affected the way in which the nation is ruled. The same lawless authority which administered the war policy with such savagery in Indochina and such deceit in America remains incumbent in the great principalities of the "second government"—the military-industrial-scientific complex—along with every other feature of the totalitarianism of advanced technocracy. The biblical mandate—in the *Letter to the Romans* no less emphatically than in the *Book of Revelation*—to resist illegitimate regimes remains as impelling and unequivocal since the end of war in Southeast Asia as it was at any moment during the open hostilities in Vietnam or the covert warfare in Cambodia and Laos. At the same time, the political effort to put a halt to this counter-revolution wrought by advanced technology and to restore political authority, lawful and accountable to human life through the constitutional system, has become more relevant and compelling than ever because of the endemic temptation to assume that the crisis is over.

It is now quite obvious that in the past quarter of a century the technological revolution has encouraged lawless authority as the real polity of the nation; that society is effectually governed by both the public and private principalities of technocracy. Common knowledge, which must in the circumstances be counted as minimal and superficial, furnishes enough evidence to boggle the imagination; the true magnitude of this new totalitarianism exceeds calculation.

—The media of technocracy, for instance, is heavily saturated with the image of a police power, engineered on a paramilitary model, relying upon technological apparatus to investigate and coerce people. It is contemptuous of both the tradition of civilian control and constitutional protection against unreasonable search and seizure, self-incrimination, detention without charge, false arrest, invasion of privacy. The common themes of this image are the glorification of official violence and the justification of police lawlessness for the sake of efficient order. These have now been repeated so often for so long that they have become accepted as the social definition of police power.

—One of our major public utilities acknowledges its practice (made possible by advanced technology) of illegally monitoring the telephone communications of at least forty million people.

—Despite bizarre and appalling disclosures of complicity in assassinations, subversion of other governments, ubiquitous oversight of citizens attempting to exercise basic political rights, usurpation of the policy-making functions of the presidency and Congress, and compilation of masses of useless, erroneous and untrustworthy intelligence data, the C.I.A. and its counterparts in practically every federal department persevere, unbeholden to public control or legal discipline.

—The great banking institutions and financial powers, whose speculations have supported the wanton proliferation of technical capacity and have converted this society to the consumption ethic, arrogantly move to abrogate representative government (or what seems to be representative government) in New York City, in a possible prelude to similar seizures in other cities.

—Though the impotence of sophisticated weaponry and the patent insanity (from a human point of view) of military overkill has been repeatedly demonstrated since the Second World War, the Pentagon remains the archetypical technocratic institution and the single most dominant ruling power. It is maintained as a law unto itself, defiant of presidential and parliamentary direction. This essential lawlessness is sustained by its enormous procurement capacity and the economy's consequent overdependence upon the Pentagon for production, trade and employment. Thus the Pentagon technocracy has achieved a near-perfect dilemma by which its political ascendancy, regardless of the Constitution, is secured: the nation must choose between insatiable waste and indefinite warfare on the one hand, and a radical loss of employment on the other.

THE PRE-EMPTION OF POLICY BY TECHNICAL CAPABILITY

In order to fully comprehend the totalitarian implications of advanced technology, one must realize the order of priorities in the policy- and budget-making processes of our society: technical capability first, human discretion second. The basic social premise, under the impact and momentum of technology, is the implementation of whatever is technologically feasible without regard to human criticism or control, and without regard to empirical benefit for human life or moral consequence for society. What is consistently involved is the intimidation or abdication of the most basic

[95]

human faculties when confronted by technological potential.

The pre-emption of policy-making—government itself—by technical capacity was exposed, symbolized grotesquely, and foreshadowed most ominously in Hiroshima. Until then scientists and politicians had often been negligent in considering the morality of their activity. But, by the time of Hiroshima, the scope of technology had so vastly expanded, diversified, and accelerated that the problem was no longer quaint or theoretical. On the contrary, it literally controlled the destiny of human life. Technical capability became the overwhelming factor in the making of policy in Hiroshima. There was a fascination with building the bomb because, as Robert Oppenheimer put it, it was so "technically sweet." The bomb was made primarily because it *could* be made; the bomb was dropped because it *could* be dropped. The facility of technology became, then and there, the factor which determined policy. It overpowered everything else, including especially the morality of building and using such a bomb.

The political implication is that policy-making becomes incorporated into the technical process itself; the participation of human beings in the exercise of rational and conscientious thought and action atrophies. Humanity becomes an adjunct to technology—robots or puppets inhibited in the use of the very faculties which distinguish them as human.

Such has become the American story. The evidence of this is everywhere: from the open commitment to genocide in Southeast Asia and the convenience of that policy for the testing of napalm, defoliation, and other weapon systems and military strategems to the profusion of wasteful, harmful, useless, redundant products and packages and the techniques of conditioning their consumption.

The issue was inadvertently if pithily expressed by David Eisenhower at an interview during the time that the Watergate scandal was becoming public knowledge. Mr. Nixon had previously remarked that the moral issue in Watergate involved those who thought "the end justified the means." (At the time he was still feigning innocence and defending his cabal as merely over-zealous in their service to him and his re-election—a cause of lofty idealism, as he construed it.) In his interview, young Eisenhower repeatedly tried to assert the same view but, in his tension, slipped, stating that the problem had to do with "the means justifying the end." Whichever aphorism might apply to Watergate, the Eisenhower dicta is fitting for American society, as it becomes a technocratic state in which technical capability surpasses all else in the determination of policy, marketing procedures, and the regime Americans must live under.

If the extraordinary political changes in American society signaled by Hiroshima had somehow taken place abruptly, in the space of a few days or weeks, it would have been recognized as the equivalent to a *coup d'état*. But the change has spanned thirty years, during which the gradual, relentless effect of technology upon people has caused little alarm and has even been considered normative. In the process, human beings have been defeated, subdued and conformed, coerced and conditioned; but the resistance to this radical dehumanization has been sporadic. One major reason for the adaptation of citizens to their own subservience to technocracy is that the metamorphosis has been accomplished without the ideological fanfare associated with other forms of totalitarianism. The technocratic state does not need ideology, in the classical sense of the word (though there is room for the argument that technology is itself an ideology), or an elaborate apparatus of propaganda and indoctrination. Rather, technology has furnished tech-nocracy with an invention capable of immobilizing human comprehension and conscience: television. There is no need for brainwashing when a machine can paralyze the mind. Television—by its sheer redundancy, by direct relay of data, and by subliminal manipulation—can hypnotize peo-ple, neutralize human response, transfix the mind. Not only does it indulge fantasy and inculcate indolence, but it habit-uates human beings to a spectator posture and to a practiced passivity which is essentially incongruous to human life. Thus, citizens are prepared for political acquiescence while remaining largely unaware of the harm done to their most basic human faculties.

THE RESISTANCE WITNESS

The transformation of American society under the impetus of technology from putative democracy to technocratic total-itarianism has long been foretold in the work of, among others, George Orwell. Orwell finds a fundamental irrecon-cilability between the political reality of advanced tech-nology and a constitutional system or rule of law such as the one familiar to Britain or America. Whether that be true as prophecy or not, the time is very late indeed in the political development of technocracy in the United States. How late it is can be seen in the situation emerging from the enfranchisement of younger voters.

Superficially, the extension of voting privileges to eigh-teen-year-old citizens seems like an opening of society to greater participation. However, these new voters, soon to constitute the potential majority of the electorate, are not even old enough to remember a society in which account-ability to human beings was esteemed. The younger voters in the United States were born and reached the age of franchise *after* the counter-revolution occasioned by technology began to gravely jeopardize the inherited constitutional ethic. At least older citizens, including those of my own generation, have a recollection of American society prior to the inception of technology when, for all its frailties and failures, there was a concern for human beings epitomized by the Bill of Rights. The eighteen-year-old voters have no such recollection; they have lived only since that concern began to be subverted and usurped by the emerging technocratic state. Why should any of these younger voters uphold the right of privacy when—in their everyday experience in school, in employment, in recreation, in travel, in credit transactions, as shoppers and consumers, in military service, in telephone or postal communications, in politics —they have known no privacy but, rather, monitoring and surveillance? The condition has become so pervasive that for the recently enfranchised young it is regarded as normative. Consequently, they have yet to be persuaded that privacy, as a human right, is both feasible and worthwhile. In this context, Orwell's views are supported: the enfranchisement of the eighteen-year-old citizens and their impending majority status in the electorate may be the empirical confirmation that technocracy is incompatible with constitutional rule.

If, in addition, the great military, scientific, and commercial principalities have significantly displaced the constitutional institutions as the functional regime, we must openly question whether suffrage has any substantial relationship to the way we are governed and policy is determined. Perhaps, in the technocratic state, elections are obsolescent and politically irrelevant—no more than an archaic ritual used to divert the attention of the people from the nation's *realpolitik*.

The view I have of the American political crisis—far

exceeding what surfaced in war and Watergate, was incipient in Hiroshima, was compounded by technology, and was institutionalized as technocracy; but that which is vested in a conglomeration of the principalities of war, science, and commerce now overtaking the constitutional system and creating a totalitarian regime which victimizes human life and brutalizes society but not public criminals or villains—is likely to be read with a foreboding that deprives Americans of hope, in a social or political sense. It should be! From a biblical point of view, the best that can be said of any such hope is that it is incredibly naive. Such hope is certain to betray those deceived by it. And, so it is not only in America today, but in any nation at any time.

What I have been describing is the doctrine of the Fall. The Fall means the profound condition of chaos and disorientation, brokenness and violence, struggle and conflict within and amongst all creatures and all things. The Fall refers to the pervasive power of death reigning throughout the whole of creation. For death to be incarnate and militant in an advanced technocratic society like America is, biblically speaking, no novelty introduced by technology, but a characteristic of every other society in every other era.

The only way for human beings to cope with the predaciousness of the technocratic regime is by comprehending, confronting, resisting, and transcending the reality of death at work in the world. It is *that* which is the whole concern of Christ's teachings. The issue is not how death can be defeated but, rather, how the power of death can be broken and confounded in the life of the word of God in this world; how human life can be emancipated from the servitude and idolatry of death in the American technocracy or in any other society whatsoever.

The biblical lifestyle is *always* a witness of resistance to the *status quo* in politics, economics, and all society. It is a witness of resurrection from death. Paradoxically, those who embark on the biblical witness constantly risk death— through execution, exile, imprisonment, persecution, defamation, or harassment—at the behest of the rulers of this age. Yet those who do not resist the rulers of the present darkness are consigned to a moral death, the death of their humanness. That, of all the ways of dying, is the most ignominious.

VII.

Evangelism, Conversion, Baptism, and Vocation

> But in fact Christ has been raised from the dead. . .
>
> *I Corinthians 15:20*

Humans are always surrounded by witnesses of the presence and vitality of death in this world: in their anxiety and loneliness; in their attempts to find identity and life, through sex; in the pursuit of success, security, and leisure through work; in fact, in all things. In the face of all that, Christians insist that the fulfillment of life—life which prevails against death and against any and every symptom of death—is in Christ, is the secret of God's work in this world.

But how does one enter into this secret? How does one receive the life constituted in the work of Christ? How does it happen that a person becomes a Christian? What does it mean to be evangelized and converted? And what does it mean to be baptized?

Perhaps no single subject excites such consternation among American Christians as that of the meaning of evangelism as related to conversion and baptism and the practice of the Christian life. In some segments of the Church, evangelism has been identified and defined in terms of a highly organized, stylized, and stereotyped transaction, in the manner of the so-called mass evangelism of Billy Graham and others. But given the high percentage of active churchpeople that flock to these crusades, one wonders whether what happens there is not evangelism at all but, rather, a form of revivalism.

Evangelism is both unwelcome outside the churches—in the marketplace, in the forums of secular life—and suppressed within many churches because churches acquiesce to that peculiar American comity that regards confessing the gospel openly or commending the gospel to another as a threat to the cohesion and tranquility of society. Evangelism is consigned at most a private and personal status; it is treated as a matter too vulgar to mention in polite public life. Probably nothing is quite so unpopular in the main-line American churches as evangelism.

Most people evidently inherit their affiliation with a church. They are baptized into church membership; they are not, for the most part, brought into the body of Christ because they have been evangelized and are converted to the Gospel.

THE MEANING OF EVANGELISM

Christians are too fond of supposing that evangelism is the work of God. I suggest that it is not. Evangelism is a task of the Church. Alongside worship and being a servant to the world, evangelism is a characteristic effort of the Church. The Church is not truly the Church if it is not engaged in all of these activities.

None of the disciples who accompanied Jesus during his historical ministry were evangelists. It is only later on— after his earthly ministry, after his crucifixion, after his descent into hell, after his resurrection, after the appearances of the risen Christ—only at Pentecost that evangelism is commissioned as an essential and characteristic enterprise of the Church. And even then there was a dispute about the nature and scope of evangelism. It is only in Peter's and the other apostles' acceptance of the authority of the evangelist Paul that evangelism is definitely and definitively regarded as a task of the Church in the world.

One suspects that sometimes evangelism is spoken of as the work of God in order to avoid the confusion that too often attaches itself to what is called evangelism; that is, the witness of the Church to the Church. Much of the activity and utterance in the churches which is said to be evangelism is, in fact, not evangelism at all but a mere witness to the Church—or some church—and an invitation to join, support, and otherwise serve a church. In any given instance that may or may not be valid and commendable practice but, whatever it may be, it is *not* evangelism.

Evangelism, as a legitimate and necessary task of the Church, is the public proclamation of the presence of the word of God in the common life of the world in a way which is accessible to all humanity for all time. Thus, evangelism always specifically refers to the extraordinary presence of the Word of God in the world in Jesus Christ.

The venerable argument as to whether or not the tactics of evangelism compel one to name the Name is answered in the fact that Jesus Christ is the historic, unique, and universal verification of God's presence in this history in the world. Jesus Christ is the assurance that all life—the life of every person and of the rest of creation—originates in and ends in the life of God. Your life, my life, or anybody's life issues from the word of God; this remains the essential truth about you, me, or anybody, no matter whatever else may be or may seem to be true.

This is of enormous practical significance in evangelism, because it means that evangelism is fundamentally an appeal to a person to remember the radical and original truth of his or her own birth and being. Evangelism does not bear the word of God to those to whom the word is utterly unknown. The evangelist merely calls upon the one addressed to recollect his or her own creation in the word of God, to remember who he or she truly is, to recover one's very own life.

Thus, evangelism is an act of love by the Church, or by a member of the Church, for the world or some person. Evangelism is the act of proclaiming the presence of the word of God in the life of another, the act of profoundly affirming that person's essential identity and being. And such an affirmation given by one to another is love.

Notice that evangelism is a very modest and simple (though not necessarily easy) task. The evangelist is not burdened with bringing the word of God *de nova* to another. For no one whom the evangelist may address is a stranger to the word of God by the evidence of her or his own life, whether he or she realizes it or not. Nor is the evangelist particularly concerned with apologetics, with defending, explaining, or arguing about the gospel. The evangelist does not really try to persuade another that the gospel is true, relevant, or objective; rather, the evangelist is engaged in loving the other in a way that calls upon the other to accept herself or himself in the same way. The evangelist is engaged in informing another person that she or he is loved by God and thus set free to be.

EVANGELISM AND CONVERSION

Evangelism is a task of the Church; conversion is a work of God. Evangelism calls upon people to remember and recognize the presence and activity of God in their own particular lives. Conversion is the event of that recall and recognition.

Put aside the unfortunate connotations that have become associated with the word *conversion*. Conversion means, simply, the event of becoming a Christian. Put aside, too, your stereotyped notions of the pattern, sequence, and accompanying signs of conversion. Consider conversion the response to evangelism; the reality of remembrance of identity which the evangelist has affirmed.

The event of becoming a Christian is the event at which a human being utterly and unequivocally confronts the presence and power of death in and over his own existence. In the same event, he is exposed to the presence and power of God overwhelming death in his own existence. Conversion is the personal experience, within the course of one's present life, of one's own death and of one's own resurrection.

It is really *death* that is involved here.

During conversion a person has a total recall of his history. All that one is and has been, all that one has done, everything that one has said, all whom one has met, every place where one has been, every fragment and facet of one's own awareness that one has been and is consigned to death, serving death, bonded to death, in fact dying. Conversion is the event during which a person finds himself radically and absolutely helpless. In becoming a Christian, a person sees that he is naked, exposed, and transparent in every respect—he is completely vulnerable. Conversion means the overpowering reality of one's *own* death, a death which one cannot resist in any fashion whatsoever. Conversion is so closely related to the presence and reality of death in the world and in one's own life in the world that on the day of the undertaker—when the body is carted away, submitted to the earth, and (with any sort of luck) honored by an obituary—on that day the one who is converted will know nothing, will suffer nothing which one has not already known and suffered in conversion, in one's death in Christ.

A person suffers his own death in conversion and, at the same time, receives the freedom from the power of death which is the resurrection. Conversion is an ultimate and radically personal exposure to death, but it is also the ultimate and immediately personal exposure to the power of God overcoming death. Conversion is death *in Christ*.

Conversion does not, characteristically, happen in a moment. It is, of course, not at all beyond God's grace to work the conversion of a person in a single moment, but there are virtually no authenticated reports of momentary conversions in the New Testament or in the history of the Church. Moreover, conversion is in itself an event that transcends the ordinary and familiar dimensions of time, for the event encompasses the whole recall of a person's biography and anticipates the end and fulfillment of a person's life eschatologically. Those who attempt to fix a specific moment as *the* moment of conversion fail to realize that conversion is the work of God in a particular person's life, not the work of the Church or an evangelist, not something sought by the one converted. Rather than regard conversion as within one moment of time, it is more fitting to consider it an event that shatters the categories of time and emancipates a person from bondage to time which is, after all, a sign of bondage to death.

The rarity of the sudden conversion (if it happens at all) is evidenced by the reports of that one conversion for which there is more information than perhaps any other conversion in the history of the Christian people—the conversion of Paul. Paul had no modesty about his conversion; his every word boasted of it. Paul's conversion was not a brief or momentary event. On the contrary, he was struck down, felled from his horse, blinded; he remained in blindness for some days and then entered and stayed in the wilderness for a long time (one account reports that it was ten years). Thereafter Paul emerged and began to practice his vocation and ministry as a Christian.

There are other significant aspects, apart from the matter of time, of Paul's conversion. For one thing, Paul's conversion was a thoroughly traumatic event; his whole being suffered the impact. He was not only physically afflicted, but he was apparently incapacitated—immobilized, so far as the usual human activities are concerned—for as long as he remained in the wilderness. The wilderness experience is integral to conversion. It is not at all a time of contemplation in the sense of the Oriental ascetics. To be in the wilderness represents a concrete encounter with death. To be in the wilderness is to be confronted with the singular reality of one's own death and the reign of death in all the world. But the wilderness is also a place into which Christ himself has come and in which Christ has already been victorious over the claims and temptations of death. Paul entered the wilderness in his conversion and beheld the triumph of Christ in the wilderness; Paul went into the wilderness and was there protected from death by Christ.

Conversion, the work of God, is truly saving in the most personal sense. There is not, as some folk vainly preach, an element of self-denial or restriction in conversion. The converted person does not denounce or give up what he was before as a person; through conversion, what he was before is restored in maturity and fulfillment. It was so with Paul who was a great zealot. Before his conversion, Paul was the most zealous persecutor of Christ. After his conversion, Paul became the most zealous evangelist and apologist. Both before and after he is still Paul the zealot. Paul is still the person he was in every sense only, now, that which he is is freed from tribute to death and fulfilled, made new, brought to mature humanity in Christ.

Thus, the work of God is conversion, a work that frees one to be the person whom the evangelist has recognized and affirms.

CONVERSION, BAPTISM, AND VOCATION

A human being who is converted will be baptized. That is, in the midst of the Church one will confess the faith; that confession will be confirmed by the Church and the members of the Church; and that person will be welcomed into the company of the Church. But what of the practice of baptism where the one baptized has not yet been converted and does not confess the faith, as is the case in infant baptism?

Such baptism is not an act of the child baptized, but an act of the Church on behalf of the child; an act in which the Church and the people of the Church, both individually and corporately, confess that they trust the gospel so much that they believe the power of God will save this child from death. The Church confesses that the grace of God, which has been sufficient to save the members of the Church, is also sufficient for this child. The Church and the members of the Church then commit themselves to raise, nurture, and love this person in such a way that he or she will come to a full maturity in Christ and later confess the faith.

Too often baptism is profaned in the churches; church-people do not realize what a radical action and responsibility is involved in baptizing a child. But the grace of God is not vitiated by the stupidity or frivolity of Christians. Even though Christians sometime invoke the name of God but do not take the matter seriously, God does. The name of God may be invoked vainly, but that name is never invoked in vain. The sufficiency of God's mercy is enough for the child even where the Church falters in its responsibility to the child, even when the people of the Church fail to love the child and his maturing in Christ.

Baptism is often profoundly misunderstood. It is widely thought to be the sacrament of the unity of the Church. But that is not what baptism is; just as it is not a mere membership or initiation ritual. Baptism is the assurance—accepted, enacted, verified, and represented by Christians—of the unity of *all humanity* in Christ. The baptized are the people in history consecrated to the unity humans receive in the worship of God. The oneness of the Church is the example and guarantee of the reconciliation of all humankind to God and of the unity of all humanity and all creation in the life of God. The Church, the baptized society, is asked to be the image of all humanity, the one and intimate community of God.

Baptism is the sacrament of the extraordinary unity

among humanity wrought by God in overcoming the power and reign of death; in overcoming all that alienates, segregates, divides, and destroys men in their relationships to each other, within their own persons, and in their relationship with the rest of creation.

Thus the vocation of the baptized person is a simple thing: it is to live from day to day, whatever the day brings, in this extraordinary unity, in this reconciliation with all men and all things, in this knowledge that death has no more power, in this truth of the resurrection. It does not really matter exactly what a Christian does from day to day. What matters is that whatever one does is done in honor of one's own life, given to one by God and restored to one in Christ, and in honor of the life into which all humans and all things are called. The only thing that really matters is to live in Christ instead of death.